The Complete Guide to ACT® Reading

Second Edition

Erica L. Meltzer

▲THE CRITICAL READER

New York

ISBN-13: 978-0-9975178-2-8
ISBN-10: 0997517824

ALSO BY ERICA MELTZER

The Complete Guide to ACT® English

The Ultimate Guide to SAT® Grammar & Workbook

SAT® Vocabulary: A New Approach (with Larry Krieger)

The Critical Reader: The Complete Guide to SAT® Reading

The Complete GMAT® Sentence Correction Guide

GRE® Vocabulary in Practice

Table of Contents

Introduction

This book is designed to overturn some of the common wisdom surrounding the ACT® Reading Test. One of the most widespread misconceptions about this portion of the exam is that it is primarily a test of speed, and is thus more or less immune to the kind of logic-based approach traditionally associated with the SAT®. Unfortunately, that is not only false but the exact opposite of the truth. In reality, a wide variety of reasoning techniques can be applied quite effectively to ACT Reading. It is true that many of those strategies require you to think and work very carefully. In some cases, they also require a great deal of self-management. But they are there, and if you use them properly, they can be exploited to great effect.

Moreover, what appear to be timing problems are often reasoning and comprehension problems in disguise. The severity of the time constraint effectively demands shortcuts. Unless you are an extraordinarily fast reader, there is simply no time to hunt through the passages for the answers to all 40 Reading questions and still finish within the allotted 35 minutes. For example, many of the most straightforward, fact-based questions only require that you locate information stated word-for-word, or nearly word-for-word, in the passage – usually not an excessively challenging task. Because these types of questions do not contain line numbers, however, you can potentially waste considerable amounts of time hunting through the passage, reading and rereading, becoming more and more panicked, and thinking less and less clearly. A vicious circle inevitably ensues. If, on the other hand, you stop and consider how the passage is organized and are able to make logical assumptions about where information is located, you are much more likely to find the information both quickly and calmly. Likewise, if you are able to stop and consider the "big picture" of a passage before plunging into the questions, you may find that you can answer some of them correctly and confidently without even looking back at the text.

Viewing ACT Reading as a task that can be approached strategically, however, often entails something of a paradigm shift. It's easy to get stuck on the idea that you should be able to read the passages and answer the questions, in order, every time. If you're accustomed to crashing through passage after passage, straining to just read a little faster and hoping that the stars will somehow align, stopping and *thinking* can seem like an unacceptable burden – not to mention an unacceptable waste of precious seconds. The problem, though, is that practice only makes perfect if it's the right kind of practice. Doing the same thing over and over again while expecting a radically different result... Well, that tends not to be very productive.

This book is therefore designed to push you out of your comfort zone and think about ACT Reading in new ways – ways that might seem very unfamiliar and perhaps even a little outrageous. But while some of those approaches may initially feel uncomfortable or counterintuitive, it is sometimes necessary for things to become harder in the short term in order for you to make progress in the long term. To be sure, though, it's a delicate balance between trying out new ways of thinking and holding on to what already works. There is no objectively "right" approach; your goal must be to find the method, or combination of methods, that is most helpful for you. Consider, then, this book as a toolbox of sorts, one that will help you to leverage your skills and apply them in the most effective way possible. Test out the various strategies presented, hold onto what works, and forget what doesn't. You are, after all, the one taking the test.

~Erica Meltzer

1 Overview of ACT Reading

The ACT Reading Test comprises five passages: three single long passages (approx. 750 words), and one set of paired shorter passages (approx. 350-375 words apiece). Each passage/passage set is accompanied by 10 questions testing content, purpose, tone, point of view, and organization, as well the ability to make logical inferences about information not explicitly stated in the text. Passages are drawn from contemporary fiction and non-fiction writings, primarily from serious books and periodicals (e.g., *Smithsonian Magazine, Scientific American, The Atlantic Monthly*) written for a general adult audience. The four passages are always presented in the same order:

1. Prose Fiction
2. Social Science
3. Humanities
4. Natural Science

Although there is an enormous amount of variation within these four categories, the passages within each one share some general characteristics and contain some recurring themes. The four categories listed above can also further be divided into two groups: Prose Fiction/Humanities and Social Science/Natural Science. There is often significant overlap between the passages in each group, in terms of content, style, and themes. Understanding this framework can help you "read the test" more effectively and recognize correct/incorrect answers more quickly and easily.

Prose Fiction/Humanities

Prose Fiction (also called **Literary Narrative**) passages are excerpted primarily from novels and short stories written within the last few decades, although excerpts from slightly older works (early twentieth century) or from works translated into English may occasionally appear as well. Passages from pre-twentieth century works do not normally appear, and you should not be concerned about having to decipher complex, Shakespearean-style writing. Prose Fiction passages are frequently written from a first-person perspective, although some are written from a third-person perspective as well. (For more information about points of view, see Chapter 10.)

In addition, Prose Fiction passages frequently contain multicultural characters/themes (African American, Native American, Hispanic, Asian American), sometimes subtly and sometimes very clearly. In the case of the latter, passages frequently focus on characters' attempts to assimilate into American society while retaining their cultural heritage. Regardless of whether the multicultural content is overt, **any passage written by a minority author or featuring members of a minority group will present the protagonist in a positive light**. Although some passages may describe familial conflict, or the challenges of living in two cultures/languages simultaneously, the majority will focus on the preservation of the characters' cultural heritage and be relatively upbeat in tone. In most cases, the relationship between the protagonist and members of older generations (e.g., parents and grandparents) will be warm and loving, and the passage will involve the transmission of values from older to younger generations.

Humanities passages differ most significantly from Prose Fiction passages in that they are always taken from non-fiction works and describe actual events. When Humanities passages are written by first-person narrators and describe important or memorable personal experiences, however, they may be virtually indistinguishable from Prose Fiction passages. The fact that they are excerpted from memoirs rather than works of fiction is essentially irrelevant. In such cases, the author's point of view is typically the same as it is in Prose Fiction passages: an adult looking back on events that occurred in their youth, or earlier in their lives, and reflecting on their meaning. At times, the language in this type of passage can be quite literary and abstract – when, for example, a writer muses on the writing process or the relationship between real life and fiction – and thus challenging to comprehend.

Humanities passages are by no means restricted to personal narratives, however. Many are written in a third-person, objective stance and describe events entirely unrelated to the author. Common topics include language and literature (especially the relationship between technology and the humanities, which will virtually always be presented in a positive way); visual arts and architecture; and music. Again, some of these more objective types of passages are minority-themed, focusing on African-American, Native American, Hispanic, and Asian-American authors, artists, and musicians, or forms of art historically associated with particular groups (e.g., jazz). Others, however, will discuss classic, well-known Western authors such as Shakespeare.

Social Science/Natural Science

Social Science (also called **Social Studies**) passages span an extremely broad range of topics, from history to linguistics to urban planning to the role of genes in determining lifespan. At one extreme, Social Science passages may seem very similar to Humanities passages; at the other extreme, they may seem nearly interchangeable with Natural Science passages, although they will rarely contain the same level of scientific terminology. As a result, they often seem less daunting, and many students find Social Science passages the most consistently straightforward and easiest to comprehend. As is true for the ACT in general, there is a strong eco-friendly tendency: recycling, bicycle shares, and solar technology = good; cars, traffic, and urban sprawl = bad.

Unlike Prose Fiction and Humanities passages, **Social Science passages are almost always written from a third-person, objective perspective.** Although the author's attitude is generally somewhat positive (why write about a subject unless you're interested in it?), the actual presentation of the information tends to be fairly neutral and factual. While some passages may be centered around an argument or claim, Social Science passages as a whole tend to be more fact- and detail-based. As a result, you should be prepared to spend a fair amount of time going to back to the passage and hunting for specific pieces of information.

Natural Science passages are primarily focused on the "hard" sciences, some familiar to most high school students (e.g., biology and chemistry), some not (e.g., astrophysics, botany, neuroscience). Unsurprisingly, the vast majority of Natural Science passages are written from a third-person, objective point of view; however, first-person narrations are not unheard of. Although these passages are often filled with technical language, some of which is likely to be very unfamiliar, it is important to understand that these passages **do not require any specialized scientific background**. Any term unlikely to be familiar to the general public will be defined; you are simply responsible for keeping track of definitions. Indeed, some questions will directly test your understanding of technical terms as they are presented in the passage. One fairly common theme is that of **"old idea" vs. "new idea."** In this model, passages will describe research that was initially controversial or viewed skeptically but that, as a result of new evidence, is now becoming more widely accepted. You can assume that questions asking about the research's original reception will have negative answers, whereas questions asking about how the work is viewed today will have positive ones.

Studying for Reading Comprehension

Aside from using *The Official ACT Prep Guide* to familiarize yourself with the test (and, of course, this book!), the most effective way to prepare for the ACT Reading Test is to regularly read the type of material that you are likely to encounter on the exam. Although this guide presents a wide variety of strategies for you to pick and choose from, the reality is that those strategies can at best allow you to make maximum use of your existing skills; they cannot substitute for a lack of comprehension or systematically expose you to a wide range of topics.

One important thing to keep in mind as you prepare is that your ability to accurately understand any given text is much more closely related to your knowledge of its topic than to your knowledge of specific reading comprehension strategies. As a matter of fact, research shows that when otherwise weak readers encounter a passage about a topic they are highly familiar with, their comprehension is actually *better* than that of strong readers with little previous knowledge of the topic.[1] In addition, the more familiar you are with a subject, the less time and energy you will have to spend trying to understand a passage about it, and the faster you'll be able to work. You'll also be familiar with specific vocabulary associated with the topic, which means you won't have to worry about keeping track of new terminology.

Moreover, you will probably find it much easier to identify correct answer choices. While you should never choose an answer simply because you know that it is factually correct, you should also keep in mind that **correct answers will always be true in the real world**. If you see an answer choice that you know is true based on your pre-existing knowledge of a topic, you can potentially save yourself a lot of time by checking that answer out first. And if you know that an answer is factually untrue, you can work from the assumption that it is wrong.

Finally, encountering a passage on a subject you already know something about can be very calming on a high-pressure test like the ACT because you will no longer be dealing with a frightening unknown. Instead of trying to assimilate a mass of completely new information in the space of a few minutes, you can instead absorb new information with relative ease, placing it in the context of your existing knowledge.

---

[1] Daniel Willingham, "How Knowledge Helps," *American Educator*, Spring 2006.
https://www.aft.org/periodical/american-educator/spring-2006/how-knowledge-helps

So does this mean that you need to spend hours daily poring over newspaper and magazine articles, trying to anticipate every possible topic that could appear on the ACT? Of course not (although spending hours reading certainly won't hurt). It does, however, mean that you should make a consistent effort to expose yourself to the type of reading you'll encounter on the exam. While the ACT is nominally a "curriculum-based" exam (a label that stuck from the early days of the exam, when factual knowledge *was* directly tested), the reality is that many ACT passages will cover topics you have never encountered in school, e.g., paleontology, string theory, and linguistics. The wider the range of information that you have been exposed to prior to the exam, the more likely you are to encounter familiar topics when you take the test for real. (The following page lists a number of publications that feature ACT-style articles, and from which ACT passages are sometimes drawn.) Setting aside even 10 or 15 minutes daily to read a couple of articles can go a long way toward improving both your comprehension and your pacing. And while the ACT does not test high-level vocabulary directly, some passages will include both challenging words and sentence structures. You should therefore make an effort to look up any unfamiliar vocabulary and to practice restating complex – and potentially confusing – constructions in your own words. You can also practice the skimming techniques outlined in the book in order to develop a good sense of how to move quickly through an unfamiliar text while still retaining the key ideas. Reading is like anything: the more you practice, the better you get.

Suggested Reading

Periodicals:

The New York Times (www.nytimes.com)
The Wall Street Journal (www.wsj.com)
Humanities Magazine (www.neh.gov/humanities)
Smithsonian Magazine (www.smithsonianmag.com)
Scientific American (www.scientificamerican.com)
Science Magazine (www.sciencemag.org)
Popular Science (www.popsci.com)
National Geographic (www.nationalgeographic.com)
The Atlantic Monthly (www.theatlantic.com)
Wilson Quarterly (www.wilsonquarterly.com)
Boston Review (www.bostonreview.net)

Books and Articles:

Temple Grandin	*Thinking in Pictures*
	Animals in Translation (with Catherine Johnson)
Ann Fadiman	*The Spirit Catches You and You Fall Down*
Brian Greene	*The Elegant Universe*
	The Hidden Reality
	The Fabric of the Cosmos
Stephen Hawking	*The Elusive Theory of Everything* (with Leonard Mlodinow)
	The Grand Design (with Leonard Mlodinow)
	A Brief History of Time
Jhumpa Lahiri	*Interpreter of Maladies*
	The Namesake
	Unaccustomed Earth
	The Lowland
National Endowment for the Arts	*Reading at Risk* (http://arts.gov/sites/default/files/ReadingAtRisk.pdf)
Steven Pinker	*The Stuff of Thought*
	How the Mind Works
	The Blank Slate
Michael Pollan	*The Botany of Desire*
	The Omnivore's Dilemma
	In Defense of Food

Oliver Sacks	*Awakenings*
	The Man Who Mistook His Wife for a Hat
	Musicophilia
	Uncle Tungsten
	Hallucinations
Amy Tan	*The Joy Luck Club*
	The Kitchen God's Wife
	The Bonesetter's Daughter
Tom Vanderbilt	"The Traffic Guru," *Wilson Quarterly*, Summer 2008.
	http://www.wilsonquarterly.com/article.cfm?AID=1234

2 Managing Time: Minimize Your Stress, Maximize Your Score

Talk to almost anyone studying for the ACT, and you'll hear the following refrain: "I know I could answer every Reading question correctly, but I always run out of time." Indeed, a significant portion of ACT Reading prep is often devoted to finding strategies for making the 35-minute time constraint more manageable. But that said, timing does not need to pose an insurmountable obstacle. Aside from the obvious fact that you must move through the Reading Comprehension section at a relatively brisk pace no matter your strategy, there are a couple of common misconceptions that add to the stress involved in working under such tight conditions: first, that it is necessary to read each passage and answer every single question, in order; and second, that time should be divided evenly among the passages, allowing you 8:45 for each one. Both of these beliefs are not only false but they also have the tendency to overshadow more helpful possibilities.

The most important thing to remember is that you can divvy up those 35 minutes and four passages any way you want. Your only goal should be to answer as many questions correctly as possible within that timeframe. Beyond that, it's up to you – you are free to pick and choose what to read and when to read it, as well as what to answer and when to answer it. Unless you are aiming for a 36, you do not have to spend time trying to answer every single question. Very often, it is not even a good idea to attempt to do so. In fact, trying to answer everything can sometimes hurt much more than it can help. Deliberately focusing the bulk of your time on the passages you understand best and the questions you are most likely to answer correctly is often a far more effective approach.

Moreover, the Reading curve is very large. Consider this: missing 8 out of a whopping 75 questions on the English Test gets you around a 29. On the Reading Test, missing 8 questions out of only *40* still gets you a 28. On some tests, you can even answer 9 or 10 questions out of 40 incorrectly and still score as high as a 28. That means you can get almost a quarter of the questions wrong and still obtain a very respectable score. Even if you're aiming for a 30+, you still have more room for error than might be expected.

Regardless of whether you can just make it through all four passages or find yourself only at the end of the third passage when time runs out, you should plan to **do the passages in order of easiest to hardest, or of most to least interesting.**

Working this way ensures that you'll pick up easy points – points that you might not get as easily if you saw those questions after struggling through a difficult passage. You won't get tired or frustrated early on, then spend the rest of the section trying to make up for the time you lost at the beginning. You might even finish the first couple of passages in less than the allotted time, meaning that you won't have to rush through the more difficult material. As a result, you'll stay calmer throughout the entire section, allowing you to actually focus on answering the questions instead of panicking about running out of time.

It is true that this strategy requires you to spend about 10-15 seconds upfront skimming the beginning of each passage and seeing which one(s) seem least painful, but it's a worthwhile tradeoff. One way to avoid having to think about which passages to start and end with, however, is to know your strengths and weaknesses. **If there's a particular type of passage that you consistently nail, do it first.** That way, you automatically start with your strongest passage without having to waste time figuring out which one that is. Likewise, **if there's a type of passage you consistently stumble on, leave it for last.** When you're struggling through those last few questions, you can console yourself with the knowledge that the section is almost over.

If you are seriously struggling with time, there are a number of possible strategies.

1) Focus on three passages and forget the fourth.

Choose your favorite three passages and focus all your time and energy on them. Instead of 8:45, you now have around 11:30 – and you can do a lot in that extra time. For the fourth passage, pick your favorite letter pair (A/F, B/G, etc.) and fill it in for every question. Statistically, you're almost always guaranteed at least two, often three, and occasionally four additional points. If you answer 10/10 correctly on the other passages, you can still score up to a 31; if you answer 9/10, you can score a 28-29; if you score 8/10, a 24, etc. That last one might not sound so great, but if you tried to answer every question and got 24 correct, you would end up with only around a 21.

This is often the most effective strategy for **very slow readers with solid comprehension skills**. If you frequently struggle with comprehension as well as timing, however, this strategy is probably too much of a risk. It can also backfire if you get an unusually difficult passage. If you answer four or five questions incorrectly on one passage and don't get everything right on the others, you can easily end up with a score in the low 20s or even the teens. And from a psychological perspective, it can be awfully nerve racking to know that you're ignoring a full quarter of the test. Admittedly, that's a risk that many people are uncomfortable with. Still, in my experience, this is **by far the best method if you cannot even come close to finishing in time**. If you stick with it long enough, eventually you'll get a score you can handle. It might not be the score you originally wanted, but it also might be one that's just high enough to make you a competitive candidate at your top-choice college. I've had more than one student use this technique to maneuver their way into a score just high enough to get their application serious consideration, then ultimately be accepted on the strength of the rest of their accomplishments at a "reach" school.

2) Do all four passages, but "skip" some questions.

This strategy tends to work best for faster readers who can *almost* finish all four passages in time. Instead of trying to answer every question, plan to fill in your favorite letter pair for one or two of the most difficult/time-consuming questions in each passage. If you forget about one question in each passage and answer everything else correctly, you can still score a 32-33; two, you can still score a 28-30; three, a 25-26, etc.

In order for this strategy to work, however, you must be truly committed to it. The primary danger is that you'll decide during the test that you want to answer every question after all, and run out of time or answer many questions incorrectly because you were racing to finish.

This strategy also requires that you be able to quickly identify the questions that are most likely to give you trouble so that you don't waste time on them. You don't want to spend a full minute working on a single question before realizing that you would have been better off skipping it. Again, it all comes down to knowing what sorts of questions are easy for you, and what sorts of questions are likely to result in wasted time and energy.

3) Do all four passages but spend more time on some, less on others.

This is another strategy that works well for strong readers who just feel a little pressed for time. If you know, for example, that Natural Science and Social Science tend to be easier for you, aim to do them in about 8:00, leaving 9:30 for Prose Fiction and Humanities. Or if you can blast through them in 7:30, you'll have 10:00 each for the remaining two. You have to play around with the proportions until you figure out what you're most comfortable with. If you get it right, the payoff can be enormous: I've seen students raise their Reading scores from a 25 to a 33 this way.

4) Answer the questions with line references as you read the passage.

If you consistently spend too much time trying to absorb the details of the passage and find yourself already running behind when you start to answer the questions, this strategy offers you a way to accomplish two things at once.

Before you begin reading the passage, glance through the questions and mark the ones that include line references.

Go to the passage, and *quickly* bracket off those lines. As long as you can tell which lines you need to focus on, this is not the time to worry about being meticulous.

Then, as you read, answer the questions whose responses are found in the lines you've bracketed. Note that sometimes you will need to read a bit above and below the line reference, but in general, answers to detail-based questions tend to be located in the lines provided.

Working this way will generally allow you answer at least three or four questions as you read the passage, allowing you to focus on only six or seven questions – rather than 10 – when you finish reading.

Important: Do not spend time bracketing the lines and then forget to answer the questions as you read! I have encountered multiple students who looked through the questions and marked line references, but then waited to answer all of the questions until they had finished reading the passage. If you do not actually answer the questions as you read, the time you spent looking over the questions and bracketing off lines will be wasted.

The Importance of Staying Flexible

To reiterate, the ACT's straightforward *style* is hardly proof that it can only be approached in the most straightforward way. The degree of strategy you want to apply, however, is up to you. **If you are uncomfortable taking risks and making quick decisions, you should form a plan and stick to it strictly.** But if you are a solid reader and enjoy thinking on your feet, you can further boost your score by adapting your strategy to the particular set of passages in front of you.

There is no single order or approach that works for everyone; it all depends on your particular strengths and weaknesses. Most people need to spend some time experimenting, and you will most likely have to try a variety of different strategies until you determine which ones are most comfortable and effective.

For example, let's say that you usually get everything right on Natural Science and sometimes on Social Science, but Humanities is all over the place, and you frequently crash and burn on Prose Fiction. Your strategy might look something like this:

1. Natural Science

2. Social Science

3. Humanities

4. Prose Fiction (SKIP if you're focusing on three passages)

On some tests, that plan might work out very well. The problem is that the content and difficulty of each passage type can vary considerably from test to test. Humanities passages can sometimes be very straightforward, and Social Science passages can be very challenging. Or Humanities can be very challenging, whereas Prose Fiction can be very straightforward. So if you're a bit more willing to think on your feet, you could also choose Option #2:

1. Natural Science

2. Social Science

3. Choose between Humanities and Prose Fiction

4. Remaining passage (or SKIP)

This way, you don't spend time on a more difficult passage and lose easy points.

And if you make snap decisions very effectively, you could even choose Option #3:

1. Natural Science

2. Choose between Social Science and Humanities

3. Chose between the remaining passage and Prose Fiction

4. Remaining passage (or SKIP)

This strategy further reduces the possibility that you will end up choosing a harder passage over an easier one.

Managing Paired Passages

New thing! find out how to deal with!!

One thing to be aware of is that in June 2014, the ACT added paired SAT-style paired passages to the Reading Comprehension Test. While three of the four passage categories still contain conventional long single passages of about 750 words, the remaining category contains two shorter passages of about 350-375 words. Both passages in a paired set will always discuss the same topic and be related to each other in some way. For example, they may present different perspectives on the same topic, or the second passage may illustrate an idea discussed in the first.

Paired passages can appear in any of the four categories, and there is no way to predict which category they will fall into on a given test. Although these passages can create a bit of a twist in terms of strategy, they need not be a significant source of concern. In general, **the paired format tends to be less important than the actual content of the passages.** If you understand a topic well when there is only one passage, you'll probably understand it well when there are two.

Keep in mind as well that only seven of the 10 questions will normally ask about the passages *separately* – only three questions will ask about the relationship between them. And questions that do ask about both passages are typically quite straightforward. Provided that you grasp the basic relationship between the passages, such questions tend to be very manageable.

If you are a strong reader across the board, you are thus likely to find that paired passage have little effect on your approach to the test (although you may want to save them for last in order to avoid a time crunch if you find that they are more time-consuming than single passages).

Even if you do consistently well only on certain passage types and are shaky on the others, you should probably stick with doing your strongest categories first – regardless of whether they are single or paired. Particularly if you are scoring in the mid-20s or higher and single passages aren't normally a problem, paired passages will most likely be fine as well.

If your comprehension is more uneven and/or you find paired passages particularly challenging, however, you may need to consider that factor when deciding what order to tackle the passages in. In some cases, the "paired" factor can actually make the decision easier because it offers a quick way of determining which passage to postpone or skip.

At the extreme, if you find paired passages so challenging that you want to avoid them regardless of what category they fall into, then you should automatically plan to leave them for last, or even guess on them, and do the remaining three passages in order of ease/interest. Likewise, if you are generally weakest in the category of the paired passages, you should automatically plan to leave them for last (or guess).

To reiterate: deciding on the spot which passages to focus on and what order to do them in won't work unless you're willing to sacrifice a few seconds choosing between passages, and can accurately gauge difficulty levels from the first few sentences. **If you get too nervous about losing time or have trouble quickly determining how difficult passages are likely to be, you're better off coming up with a clear plan well in advance and sticking to it when you take the test.** You might not reach your target score on the first try, but if you play to your strengths long enough, you stand a good chance of getting there eventually.

Using Time Effectively on Each Passage/Question Set

In addition to having a plan for managing your time on the entire section, you should also have a general plan for managing your time on each individual passage/question set.

It is extremely common for students to run out of time on the Reading Test not because they spend a little too much time doing everything, but rather because they do almost everything at a reasonable clip and then get bogged down doing a few exceptionally time-consuming tasks – most often, either reading the same confusing section of a passage over and over, or hunting through the passage for a detail that just doesn't want to be found. One of your primary challenges, then, is to resist the temptation to "fight" with these sections/questions. Refusing to give up on a question may be rewarding psychologically, but when it comes to finishing the questions in the allotted time, it's just about the worst thing you could do.

I do not, however, generally advocate skipping the passage and jumping directly to the questions. Although this approach does save time in the short term, it can actually be more time-consuming in the long run. Because you will lack any sense of context when you look at the questions, you will often spend *more* time hunting for answers that you could otherwise determine in a couple of seconds, given a general understanding of the passage.

The only **exception** is as follows: If you choose to focus your attention primarily on three passages and happen to have three or four minutes left over after working through everything else carefully, you can try to grab a few easy-looking questions from the remaining passage. Since you are usually statistically guaranteed at least two questions just from random guessing, however, you are probably better off spending that time working on questions that accompany a passage you've actually read.

The fact that you should not skip passages entirely does not, however, mean that you need to pore over every word. **In fact, you should read each passage as quickly as possible without sacrificing comprehension.** There's no point in speeding through if you're going to look up at the end and wonder what you just read.

Your goal during the initial read-through is to obtain a general **idea of what the passage is about, how it's organized, and where the important information is located. You should never try to absorb every last detail. If you find part of the passage confusing, skip it and focus on what you do understand.** The last thing you want to do is waste a minute reading and rereading a sentence that might at most be relevant to a single question.

You should also make sure that you finish each passage with enough time left over to answer all of the questions you intend to answer. If you're planning to do all four passages, you should spend no more than about 2-2:30 reading. If you're doing three passages, aim to finish in about 3-3:30. **Remember: you can and should go back to the passage in order to search for the details as you work through the questions.** Even if you read the passage slowly, your mind simply cannot store its contents fully after one read-through, especially when you're under pressure. You'll almost certainly have to go back to the passage, no matter how slowly you read it the first time.

Working through the questions is a little trickier, and the amount of skipping around you are willing to do will of course depend on your ability to judge which questions/question types are most likely to give you trouble, as well as your level of comfort with working out of order. **Your goal is to avoid sacrificing questions that you could answer both quickly** and easily in order to spend time on ones that you may or may not get right. Basically, if something looks hard and complicated, save it for later. There are times when procrastination can be a good thing, and this is one of them.

Regardless of how comfortable you are with skipping around, a good rule of thumb is that if you look at a question and your immediate reaction is *Huh???*, you're probably better off skipping it for the time being. In addition, **certain types of questions – particularly inference; all of the following EXCEPT; I, II, and III; and detail-based questions without line references – are often impossible to do quickly, no matter how strong a reader you are.** If you encounter one of these questions early on in a section and either aren't sure of the answer or have no clear idea of how to start working toward the answer within the first few seconds, you're probably better off leaving it and coming back to it once you've answered everything you can answer quickly. **If you're worried you won't remember to come back to the questions you've skipped, mark them with a huge star or circle.** Just don't cheat yourself out of easy points.

You also have to know when it's worth it to let things go. If you've worked through nine questions in a set and are still struggling through #10 when your time runs out for that passage, either leave the question to come back to after you're done with the rest of the Reading Test, or bubble in your most reasonable guess. **You cannot afford to get behind on the other passages for the sake of a single question.**

3 Reading Fast and Slow

If you ask those rare lucky people who can easily complete all four passages in time how they finish so quickly, they'll probably just shrug and tell you that they're just reading the passages and answering the questions. What most highly skilled readers often do not recognize, though, is that their "naturally" fast reading is actually the result of a combination of specific skills. But because expert readers generally take those skills for granted, performing them subconsciously, they can't explain what those skills are, never mind explain to someone else how to acquire and apply them. The good news, however, is that those skills can be learned. You probably won't turn into a champion speed-reader overnight, but you can learn to read more quickly as well as more effectively.

Brute speed, no doubt, is very effective for ACT Reading, but it is not the whole story. In reality, **the key to finishing Reading Comprehension in the allotted time is not simply to read quickly but to read efficiently**. If you understand how passages are organized and can summarize them effectively, you can often use a general, "bird's eye" understanding to answer three or four questions without even looking back, leaving you plenty of time to hunt for the answers to those pesky little detail questions that you do need to search for.

One of the biggest mistakes that people make when reading ACT passages is to assume that all sentences deserve equal attention. As a result, when they encounter something they don't understand, they figure it must be important and read it again. And if they still don't understand it, they it read again. And maybe even a third and fourth time. Before they know it, they've spent almost a minute reading and rereading a single sentence. When they finally move on, they're not only confused and frustrated (which makes it harder to concentrate on the rest of the passage) but they've also lost sight of what the passage is actually about.

What's more, when most people skim through a passage, they simply try to read *everything* faster, with the result that they don't understand the passage as more than a string of vaguely related sentences. As a result, they lack a sense of the big picture when they look at the questions. Because they haven't focused on the key places indicating the passage's main ideas and concepts, they're often perplexed when they encounter big-picture questions that ask them to think about the passage as a whole. And because they've just been worrying about each individual piece of information as they encounter it, they have trouble thinking about where information would logically be located for detail-based questions.

Skimming effectively, on the other hand, means reading selectively. Some sections are read very slowly, while others are glanced through or even skipped over entirely. Reading this way requires much more thought and focus, but it is also much faster and, when done properly, can actually improve comprehension. In order to know what to read slowly and what to skip, however, you must be able to recognize which types of information are important and which types are not.

How to Skim Effectively

As you're probably beginning to notice, the type of reading that the ACT requires you to do is very different from the type of reading you are assigned in school. Whereas your English teacher probably wants you to read as carefully as possible, perhaps even asking you to provide detailed annotations, the ACT requires that you gain a general understanding of the passage as quickly and efficiently as possible. Practically speaking, that means your job is to hunt for the key points of the passage, creating a general "map" of them for yourself so that you can go back and locate the details as necessary while you answer the questions. In general, the most effective way to create such a map is to combine your knowledge of key textual elements (transitions, punctuation, strong language) and paragraph organization to know when to slow down and when to speed up. Doing these things requires that you read much more actively – that you pay attention not only to the words you are reading at any particular moment, but also consider how those words fit into the passage as a whole.

As a general rule, you should always make sure to carefully read the introduction (usually only the first paragraph, but occasionally the first two or even three paragraphs), focusing particularly on the last sentence or two. In addition you should always read the conclusion (last paragraph) slowly, paying close attention to the last sentence. These two places essentially serve as "anchors" for the passage: the purpose of the introduction is to tell you what the passage is about – to set up the primary ideas or questions it will discuss – and the purpose of the conclusion is to reiterate the main idea of the passage and explain its larger importance. If you find yourself getting lost in the details, reading or rereading these places can help you re-focus and understand why the author has included other pieces of information.

As you read through the passage, you should also **pay close attention to the beginning and end of each paragraph.** Sometimes it will be enough to read the first sentence, and sometimes you will need to read two or three sentences in to figure out what the paragraph is about and where it's heading. Once you have a good idea of those things, however, you can often jump to the last sentence or two of the paragraph.

In addition, you should try to notice any major changes in topic, focus, or point of view. For example, the first few paragraphs of some passages may be written in the first person (*I*), then switch into the third person (*he/she/it*). Other passages may devote the first few paragraphs to describing a general situation and then use the remainder of the body paragraphs to discuss a specific example or series of examples. Questions may sometimes explicitly ask about where these shifts occur; in such instances, being able to "chunk" a passage into sections will help you more quickly identify where key information is located.

Finally, you should pay attention to **major transitions, strong language, and "interesting" punctuation** such as a colons, semicolon, dashes, and quotation marks. Words and phrases such as *therefore, for example, however, because* and *in fact* tell you when authors are drawing conclusions, offering supporting evidence, shifting directions, and emphasizing key points. Very often, the information you need to answer questions will be located near these words. (For a complete list of things to circle, see p. 25.) On the other hand, you should generally avoid circling or underlining **nouns**, including proper names. Although this may seem counter-intuitive – wouldn't the author only mention a person if they were important? – nouns themselves tell you nothing about *why* those names, things, or places are important, only that they are in some way relevant to the topic at hand.

The chart on p. 25 provides a list of punctuation marks and phrases to look out for as you read. Although the list may seem quite extensive, it is important not to try to turn the reading process into a transition hunt. You do not need to compulsively circle every *and* and *but* that you encounter. Rather, the goal is to help yourself identify the most important information by noticing the "signals" that alert you to its presence. Essentially, you can think of these words and punctuation marks as the literary equivalent of traffic signals: they tell you when to speed up, when to slow down, and when to pay close attention. They also eliminate the need to underline large blocks of text – when you underline too extensively, you can easily lose sight of what's actually important. In contrast, focusing on transitions allows you to put information in context and understand *why* it matters.

Important: If you find that looking out for transitions while you read seriously interferes with your ability to absorb the meaning of a passage, you are better off not attempting to circle them when you do an **initial** read-through. Under no circumstances should you sacrifice comprehension in favor of rigid adherence to a strategy. That does not, however, mean that you should ignore transitions completely. When you go back to the passage as you answer the questions, you should still make sure to pay careful attention to them. Often, key information will be located close by – information that you would otherwise be likely to overlook.

Also: as you skim, you should make sure to put your finger on the page and move it along the line as you read. (You should not, however, follow along with the tip of your pencil so that you end up underlining the entire passage as you read. Underlining everything is the same as underlining nothing.) Using your finger this way allows you to have a physical connection to the text. It focuses your mind and your eye, making it easier for you to notice key pieces of information that you might otherwise not notice.

Key Words and Punctuation

Continuers		Contradictors
Add Information	**Speculate**	But
		However
And	If	Yet
Furthermore	May	(Al)though
Moreover	Maybe	On the contrary
In addition	Might	On one hand/
Also	Could	On the other hand
As well as	Perhaps	In contrast
First	It is possible	Whereas
In the first place		While
Second	**Emphasize**	Despite
Next		In spite of
Then	Indeed	Nevertheless
Finally	In fact	Meanwhile
For example	Let me be clear	Instead
For instance	Italics	Still
One/another reason	Capital letters	Rather than
	Exclamation point	Misguided
Draw a conclusion	Repetition	False
So	**Indicate Importance**	**Question**
Therefore		
Thus	Important	But is it really true…?
Thereby	Significant	Question mark
As a result	Essential	Quotation marks
	Fundamental	
Compare	Principal	
	Central	
Similarly	Key	
Like/likewise	Point	
As	Goal	
Just as	Purpose	
Much as/like	(Main) idea	
Explain/Define		
Because		
The reason/answer is		
That is why		
That is to say		
Colon		
Dash		

Now look at the passage on the next page, and observe how these elements can be used to help you identify a handful of key places in a passage.

"A finite universe"—that's the phrase that Jim Kuhn uses to describe the surviving early quartos of Shakespeare's plays. It evokes something that seems more expansive and dynamic than the estimated 777 paperback-sized volumes that, for the last four hundred years, have physically carried our most direct evidence of the Bard's work. **It also begins to suggest the appeal of those volumes in aggregate: There is an end to their universe, the texts that define it can be collected, and that collection, completed.**

Five years ago, Kuhn, then head of collection information services at the Folger Shakespeare Library, helped to prototype just such a **collection: a** digital repository capable of bringing together in one location the sparse and geographically scattered universe of these rare Shakespeare texts. The project, which was led by the Folger and the University of Oxford, involved librarians, curators, computer scientists, educators, and interns from scholarly institutions on both sides of the Atlantic.

As a proof of concept, they tackled the thirty-two early copies of *Hamlet* held by the participating libraries (the Folger, the British Library, the Bodleian Library at Oxford, the Huntington Library, the National Library of Scotland, and the University of Edinburgh Library). Sixteen months spent gathering cover-to-cover digital images, producing transcriptions, and developing an online interface resulted, in November of 2009, in the Shakespeare Quartos Archive, which boasts the **most comprehensive** collection of early *Hamlets* available and is setting an example for newer literary archives such as the recently announced Shelley–Godwin Archive.

Among Shakespeare's works, *Hamlet* is an **obvious choice** for such an endeavor, **not only** because of the play's iconic status in literary and popular culture, **but because** many perplexities surround its textual transmission. "*Hamlet* goes from the stage to the printed page at one point or another," says Steven Galbraith, another former member of the SQA's Folger team; "**but** the printed page is, materially, what survives for us." We don't have an authorial manuscript (of Hamlet or any of the Bard's works) against which to judge those pages, and, as it turns out, we don't have an unassailably stable *Hamlet* in any form: We have *Hamlets*, **plural**—a circumstance that becomes amply clear when one turns to the surviving quartos themselves. Look closely enough, and not just every edition, **but** every copy differs from every other.

Helping readers get a good look at these quartos is where the SQA **excels**. Partnering with yet another scholarly institution (the Maryland Institute for Technology in the Humanities, which is part of the University of Maryland, College Park), the SQA team developed a web-based interface and set of digital tools designed for close, almost microscopic, comparative analysis. Among a number of other features, one can execute word searches on the texts, superimpose and adjust the transparency of page images, and run a difference algorithm that immediately highlights every **inconsistency—including** printers' marks, marginal notations, and other paratextual **matter—between** any two of the archive's scrupulously executed transcriptions. Armed with these tools, the **"originals"** can begin to look like a dense patchwork of **inconsistency**—*Hamlet*, hopelessly at odds with itself.

Galbraith, a curator by trade, has **another perspective** on the body of evidence that the SQA offers up, one that looks beyond the *Hamlet* texts themselves, to their **value** as archaeological specimens. "Every book has its own story," he says, "and using the SQA with a critical eye, you can really begin to see that. There are differences in bindings, different people have owned them and marked them up, used them in different ways." **And the bigger question, he adds, the one to which all these differences lead, is one of provenance: "Where has this book been for the last four hundred years?"** Tracing the hand or characteristic markings of some previous reader through the text, focusing on the passages or words that he or she focused on, identifying the binder or the most worn pages, one can begin to piece together the trajectories of these individual books through history and how they were used.

The SQA's collection of high-resolution and transcribed *Hamlets* may, with some clever detective work, prove a boon to literary scholars and bibliographers. **But, as both Kuhn and Galbraith point out, the archive also helps to raise and answer questions touching on digitization efforts beyond Shakespeare: What do you do when the imaging and transcription are done? What can you do with the texts now that you couldn't do before?** Neither the content of the **plays—the** lines, words, punctuation marks, paratextual matter, **marginalia—nor** the images of their physical medium necessarily suggest all of the uses to which the data might be put. Making the texts accessible, and, what is **more important**, accessible as data, opens them up to modes of analysis and creativity beyond those traditionally associated with the humanities. "**The goal,**" says Galbraith, "is to release that data and let the scholars, directors, and artists, or whoever is coming to the quartos, do their work with them in whatever way, for whatever reason." One wonders what a statistician, digital artist, or data visualization expert might find in the SQA.

Skimming Paragraphs

As you most likely learned back in elementary school, paragraphs consist of two basic elements: introductory material (topic sentence that presents the paragraph's topic and purpose) and supporting evidence (specific examples). Paragraphs in ACT passages can be organized in a variety of ways, but many of them will follow this essential structure. This is good news for you because paragraphs organized this way are exceptionally easy to skim; during an initial read-through, you often will not even need to read past the first sentence or two. If you recognize that the bulk of the paragraph is simply there to support the main idea of the paragraph, you have no reason to slog through the details.

Sometimes the author will provide a transition such as *for instance* or *for example*, which clearly indicates that the following information is there to provide supporting evidence. In such cases, you know immediately that you can skim through (or even skip) that section. Other times, however, authors will not spell out for you that they're providing an example. Instead of saying *for example* or *for instance*, they'll simply launch into the supporting evidence. What that is the case, you must use your knowledge of paragraph organization to recognize what you can skip.

For example, consider the following paragraphs. Main ideas are in bold.

Example #1:

European zoos of the late 19th and early 20th centuries incorporated the visual cultures of their animals' native homes into ornate buildings — reflections of their nations' colonial aspirations. The Berlin Zoo's ostrich house resembled an Egyptian temple, with large columns flanking the entrance and scenes of ostrich hunts decorating the exterior. Berlin's elephant enclosure was built in the spirit of a Hindu temple; the home for its giraffes adopted an Islamic architectural style. Zoos in Cologne, Lisbon, Antwerp, and Budapest, among others, created similar exhibits. **These zoos were no home for subtlety: The animals they contained were exotic to most visitors; the buildings that did the containing reinforced the sensation.**

You can find similar nods to foreign cultures in some U.S. zoos. The Cincinnati Zoo's Taj Mahal-like elephant house, **for example,** and its pagoda-like Passenger Pigeon Memorial Hut are both National Historic landmarks. In *Animal Attractions: Nature on Display in American Zoos*, historian Elizabeth Hanson compares the style of the National Zoo's Reptile House to that of northern Italy's Romanesque cathedrals — an appropriation that gave the building more than just an appealing look.

Both of these paragraphs are stellar examples of the topic sentence/supporting evidence structure. Each consists of a single topic sentence (bold) that states the main idea of the paragraph, and is followed by specific examples that clearly illustrate the topic sentence's claim. There is, however, one important difference between the paragraphs. Notice that in the second paragraph, the transition *for example* indicates that the information that follows is there to support the main idea (buildings in U.S. zoos contain foreign elements). As a result, you know immediately that it is not necessary to closely read the information that follows.

In contrast, the first paragraph simply moves into a series of examples, immediately following the topic sentence. In that case, you are responsible for making the connection between the words *European zoos* at the start of the paragraph, and *Berlin Zoo* at the start of the second sentence. Since Berlin is a city in Europe, you can infer that the author is giving a specific example of a zoo that *incorporate[d] the visual culture of the animals' native homes into ornate buildings*. If you look ahead in the paragraph, you can see that other cities (Cologne, Lisbon, etc.) are mentioned as well. Logically, those sentences simply extend the series of examples and do not need to be read closely.

If you wanted to go through the two paragraphs as quickly as possible, you could therefore read only each topic sentence. There is, however, one piece of "interesting" punctuation worth noticing in the last sentence of each paragraph: a colon (first paragraph) and a dash (second). At this point, it is not worth your time to stop and ponder the significance of the sentences that contain them those punctuation marks. On the other hand, it is worth your time to take a half-second and circle that colon and dash. Ideally, you should also underline or bracket the sentence that contains it. Even if you do not yet know why the information is important, there is a good chance that it will contain the answer to a question, and it is therefore worth reminding yourself to pay attention to it.

So to recap: while those two paragraphs appear to contain a fair amount of information, it is possible to get the gist by reading only this:

> European zoos of the late 19th and early 20th centuries incorporated the visual cultures of their animals' native homes into ornate buildings — reflections of their nations' colonial aspirations. ~~The Berlin Zoo's ostrich house resembled an Egyptian temple, with large columns flanking the entrance and scenes of ostrich hunts decorating the exterior. Berlin's elephant enclosure was built in the spirit of a Hindu temple; the home for its giraffes adopted an Islamic architectural style. Zoos in Cologne, Lisbon, Antwerp, and Budapest, among others, created similar exhibits.~~ These zoos were no home for subtlety: The animals they contained were exotic to most visitors; the buildings that did the containing reinforced the sensation.
>
> You can find similar nods to foreign cultures in some U.S. zoos. The Cincinnati Zoo's Taj Mahal-like elephant house, for example, ~~and its pagoda-like Passenger Pigeon Memorial Hut are both National Historic landmarks. In~~ *~~Animal Attractions: Nature on Display in American Zoos,~~* historian Elizabeth Hanson compares the style of the National Zoo's Reptile House to that of northern Italy's Romanesque cathedrals — an appropriation that gave the building more than just an appealing look.

Or even this:

> European zoos of the late 19th and early 20th centuries incorporated the visual cultures of their animals' native homes into ornate buildings — reflections of their nations' colonial aspirations. ~~The Berlin Zoo's ostrich house resembled an Egyptian temple, with large columns flanking the entrance and scenes of ostrich hunts decorating the exterior. Berlin's elephant enclosure was built in the spirit of a Hindu temple; the home for its giraffes adopted an Islamic architectural style. Zoos in Cologne, Lisbon, Antwerp, and Budapest, among others, created similar exhibits. These zoos were no home for subtlety: The animals they contained were exotic to most visitors; the buildings that did the containing reinforced the sensation.~~
>
> You can find similar nods to foreign cultures in some U.S. zoos. The Cincinnati Zoo's Taj Mahal-like elephant house, for example, ~~and its pagoda-like Passenger Pigeon Memorial Hut are both National Historic landmarks. In~~ *~~Animal Attractions: Nature on Display in American Zoos,~~* ~~historian Elizabeth Hanson compares the style of the National Zoo's Reptile House to that of northern Italy's Romanesque cathedrals — an appropriation that gave the building more than just an appealing look.~~

At this point, you might be thinking that this is a very unnatural way to read, and that there's no way you could ever make sense out of anything that way. And to be perfectly frank, that might be the case. Jumping from key idea to key idea can feel like a very unnatural way to read, and this technique will not work for everyone. But remember: if you want to improve, you have to be willing to push yourself out of your comfort zone. And if you can't finish in time, you don't have anything to lose trying. If you spend some time every day actively practicing reading this way, you might be surprised at how quickly you pick it up. Initially, though, you will probably find it requires more focus than what you are accustomed to.

Example #2

Now let's try an exercise. Read the following sentence, and see whether you can determine what information the rest of the paragraph will contain.

> When the framers of the Constitution made their document public on September 17, 1797, after four long months of closed deliberation, they tacked on a string of non-negotiable demands. They insisted...

Because the author refers to what *they insisted* upon after the phrase *string of non-negotiable demands*, you can reasonably assume that the paragraph will go on to list those demands. And in fact, that is exactly what happens. Now read the whole paragraph:

> When the framers of the Constitution made their document public on September 17, 1797, after four long months of closed deliberation, they tacked on a string of non-negotiable demands. They insisted that their document be submitted unchanged by Confederation authorities to the states for ratification, that it be approved through state conventions for that purpose rather than through the existing state legislature, that ratifications require only a strong majority of the states rather than the unanimity stipulated under the original compact, and that their own deliberations remain secret and inviolable during debate over the document that they had written. Finally, the framers resisted any reconsideration by a comparable deliberative body of the kind that they had just conducted among themselves.

It's pretty dense, right? You also might not have understood every word and phrase perfectly, and you almost certainly couldn't spit back an impromptu summary. Since you "previewed" the information by reading the topic sentence, however, you can at least understand that the paragraph is there to provide a list of non-negotiable demands made by the Constitution's framers. That might not seem like much, but if you encountered this paragraph in the middle of a passage and started to get caught up trying to absorb every word, you could more easily push yourself to jump ahead.

Example #3

Sometimes the structure of a paragraph will be less clear-cut. Authors won't always go out of their way to signal that the paragraph is organized as a claim followed by specific details. Sometimes you'll have to read a few sentences into the passage in order to recognize that you're just dealing with supporting information. It's worth paying attention to whether the information you're reading has this purpose, though. If it's only there to reiterate a point you already know, you can ignore it for the moment and jump ahead until you spot the next major transition.

For example, consider the following paragraph:

> **The southern plains could have stayed what they always had been: an expanse of grass—one hundred million acres of buffalo grass, western wheatgrass, blue grass, and hundreds of other species.** That was what the environment could support, flora-wise. Semiarid, constantly windy, and prone to droughts—with long dry spells coming along every twenty years or so—the grasses were what kept the land together, what kept it from deteriorating into outright desert. Their tangled roots held the topsoil in place, prevented it from blowing away and exposing the dense layer of hardpan underneath. **But so much rich earth, left to the good graces of nature, is hard to resist. And in the late nineteen-teens and throughout the twenties, the grass was dug up and plowed over and the churned soil left behind planted in wheat, a booming crop at the time. It was, as Oliver Edwin Baker of the Bureau of Agricultural Economics put it in 1923, "the last frontier in agriculture:" sodbusting** the ancient Plains for a buck—and there were plenty of takers.

The first sentence does actually provide a clue to where the paragraph is going, but it's a very subtle one. By stating that *The southern plains could have stayed what they had always been*, the author is implying that that the southern plains did not in fact stay what they had always been, and that the paragraph will go on to explain what they became. **Your goal for the paragraph is thus to answer the question "what happened to the plains?"**

Instead of immediately describing what happened to the plains, however, the author simply begins describing their original characteristics…and continues to do so for the next few sentences. This starts to become apparent by the third sentence (*Semiarid, constantly windy*, etc.). At this point, you can start to hunt for the next major transition – the place where the focus changes, or where new information is introduced.

That doesn't happen until the seventh line, where the transition *but* serves as a big flashing light that tells you to slow down. The following sentence also begins with a transition, *and*, suggesting that this couple of sentences will contain very important information. Sure enough, this is where the author finally explains what happened to the plains: they were *dug up and plowed over and the churned soil left behind planted in wheat, a booming crop at the time*. The sentence after that is not only the final sentence of the paragraph but it also contains both a colon and a dash, suggesting that it is extremely important.

What the skimmer actually reads therefore amounts to only about half of the paragraph.

> The southern plains could have stayed what they always had been: an expanse of grass—one hundred million acres of buffalo grass, western wheatgrass, blue grass, and hundreds of other species. ~~That was what the environment could support, flora-wise. Semiarid, constantly windy, and prone to droughts—with long dry spells coming along every twenty years or so—the grasses were what kept the land together, what kept it from deteriorating into outright desert. Their tangled roots held the topsoil in place, prevented it from blowing away and exposing the dense layer of hardpan underneath.~~ **But** so much rich earth, left to the good graces of nature, is hard to resist. **And** in the late nineteen-teens and throughout the twenties, the grass was dug up and plowed over and the churned soil left behind planted in wheat, a booming crop at the time. It was, as Oliver Edwin Baker of the Bureau of Agricultural Economics put it in 1923, "the last frontier in agriculture": sodbusting the ancient Plains for a buck—**and** there were plenty of takers.

Reading less makes it much easier to get the gist of the paragraph: the plains changed because their land could be used to grow profitable crops. Nothing from the description in the first few sentences is even relevant.

Example #4

Now let's try something even more challenging. The following paragraph is something that you could easily encounter in a Humanities passage. Take a moment to read it, and **time yourself**. Don't try to speed through it; just read at a normal pace.

> Inventing a language is arduous, and no one attempts it without a serious purpose. As Suzanne Romaine, one of the world's leading linguists, argues in *From Elvish to Klingon: Exploring Invented Languages*, "A similarity of purpose and motivation drives inventors of all new languages, whether in the real or fictional world. The perceived need for them arises from dissatisfaction with the current linguistic state of affairs. Recognition that language can be used for promoting or changing the social, cultural, and political order leads to conscious intervention and manipulation of the form of language, its status, and its uses." The quality of that dissatisfaction, however, and the language in which it's reflexively expressed, is particular to the case. We are probably all dissatisfied to some extent with the language we're given. The question is, What do our responses say about the human condition?

By ACT standards, this passage is definitely on the harder side, although still within the bounds of the test. You might run into some trouble summarizing it, though. The quote in particular has the potential to be very confusing; there's a pretty decent chance you won't know precisely what Suzanne Romaine means by *the current linguistic state of affairs* or *the conscious intervention and manipulations of the form of language.*

You might have reread those phrases multiple times, trying to make sense out of them and wasting precious seconds in the meantime. In other words, it's likely that you got caught up in the details to some extent, worrying about what you didn't understand and ignoring more straightforward information that could have helped you decipher the rest of the paragraph. That's an entirely normal response to that type of phrasing, and choosing to temporarily ignore it is probably the exact opposite of what you want to do. The problem is that the more times you read those few sentences, the more panicky you'll get, and the less you'll end up understanding.

Now try this version of the paragraph. Time yourself on it as well.

> Inventing a language is arduous, and no one attempts it without a **serious purpose**. As Suzanne Romaine, one of the world's leading linguists, argues ~~in *From Elvish to Klingon: Exploring Invented Languages*, "A similarity of purpose and motivation drives inventors of all new languages, whether in the real or fictional world. The perceived need for them arises from dissatisfaction with the current linguistic state of affairs. Recognition that~~ language can be used for promoting or changing the social, cultural, and political order ~~leads to conscious intervention and manipulation of the form of language, its status, and its uses." The quality of that dissatisfaction, however, and the language in which it's reflexively expressed, is particular to the case.~~ We are probably all dissatisfied to some extent with the language we're given. The question is, What do our responses say about the human condition?

The above version is more or less what an expert skimmer would read. A lot easier, not to mention a lot faster, right? Notice that virtually all of the most confusing information has been eliminated. There's no chance to get bogged down.

But you're probably wondering how on earth anyone could possibly know what to read and what to skip in a passage that dense and confusing. In comparison to the other examples, there are comparatively few transitions that tell you what to pay attention to.

Well, we're going to slow the skimmer's process down and examine it in very, very slow motion. In reality, these steps would be performed in a matter of seconds. But if we were to separate out the principle steps of the process, they would go something like this:

First, the skimmer would read the first sentence slowly. The purpose of the first sentence is to tell the reader what the paragraph is about, so it always deserves special attention.

Inventing a language is arduous, and no one attempts it without a <u>serious purpose</u>.

Now, the skimmer pauses for a fraction of a section, considering what that sentence suggests about the rest of the paragraph. If an author states that *no one attempts to [invent a language] without a serious purpose*, then logically, that author is going to spend the rest of the paragraph discussing why people invent languages. That's the purpose of the paragraph. So now the skimmer's goal for the rest of the paragraph is to find the reason that people invent languages.

With that in mind, the skimmer then notices that the next sentence introduces a quotation by an expert in the field (*As Suzanne Romaine, <u>one of the world's leading linguists,</u> argues…*). Why include a quotation? To support the point. What's the point? Inventing a language is serious business. Looking through the quote, the reader searches for the **clearest, most specific reason** that people invent languages, and finds it about halfway through (*promoting or changing the social, cultural, and political order*).

Having found the answer to the paragraph's central question, the skimmer can skip to the end. The last sentence is a question, and questions are usually important, so the skimmer slows down there as well. Like the topic sentence, the last sentence "previews" what will come next. By asking *what…our responses say about the human condition?* the author suggests that he will probably address the question in the next paragraph.

4 "Mapping" the Passage

Knowing how to skim paragraphs is important, but just as important – if not more so – is knowing how to skim passages as a whole. Although one skill leads naturally to the next, there are some additional elements to take into account when looking at large blocks of text.

The first thing to do during an initial read-through is to identify what type of passage you're dealing with: personal narrative or objective, third-person description? Is the author arguing a point, or is the passage more descriptive and detail-based? ACT passages can be either, and Prose Fiction aside, there is no way to consistently predict which type of passage will be which. As a result, you need to be prepared to adjust your focus slightly depending on which category a particular passage falls into. If the passage – or part of the passage – has a clear point, you need to look out for examples (and counterexamples). Once you know where sections are located and what role they play in the argument, you may be able to skim through them. If a passage is more descriptive, however, you may need to slow down and read more carefully. Important information will not always be presented in the expected places (introduction, beginnings/ends of paragraphs). Until you figure out what's going on, you will have to pay close attention.

One important skimming strategy is to look for the **major sections** within the passage. Typically, the text can be separated into two or three large chunks, in which different aspects of the topic are discussed, or shifts in point of view occur. If it helps you, you can bracket off those sections to have a visual cue for how the passage is arranged. Having a clear idea of what each section discusses will focus you and make it less necessary for you to read every word. And if you encounter a question that asks you where a shift in the passage occurs, you can probably jump right to the answer.

Like paragraphs, entire passages often move from **general** to **specific**. The author may devote the first paragraph or two to describing a general situation or topic, then shift to providing specific examples. In the conclusion, the author will typically shift back to a more general discussion, "opening up" the topic and explaining its larger significance.

When an author is discussing a topic **in general**, you will usually see lots of **plural nouns** and/or references to a **category or type of thing** (e.g., *books*).

When the author moves to a more **specific** discussion and/or provides examples, you will usually see references to a **particular person or things**. As a result, you will see **proper names and singular nouns** that refer to specific things (e.g., *William Shakespeare*, *the* book). **The section changes when the shift from general to specific (or vice versa) occurs.**

The passage on the following page follows that general structure. Words that indicate general and specific are in **bold**.

Section 1

A barn. A warehouse. A closet. These locations have something in common: They all contained **films** or parts of **films** that were missing and presumed lost forever. According to reliable estimates, at least 50 percent of all films made for public exhibition before 1950 have been lost. Move into the silent era, and the estimate shoots up to 90 percent. The cellulose nitrate film on which **movies** were recorded until 1950 is flammable and highly susceptible to deterioration. The medium that replaced nitrate, cellulose acetate, solved the flammability problem, but is vulnerable to disintegration, shrinkage, and breakage.

Film needs to be stored in a temperature and moisture controlled environment. **Film archives** all over the world maintain such climate-controlled storage facilities as a first line of defense. Transferring nitrate film to stable safety stock is a second precaution **film preservationists** take.

Actual restoration is a further, complicated step that many films will never undergo. Restoring celluloid **films** is a costly, time-consuming process that requires expert handling in one of the few photochemical labs that still exist; today, more **films** are being restored through digital correction, but this work is also labor-intensive.

The work also requires old-fashioned research. **Film** is an art form that everyone from producers to theater owners has felt entitled to alter to fit their requirements, including shortening **films** to maximize the number of screenings and cutting out material the exhibitor deemed inappropriate. Therefore, research must be done to find shooting scripts, directors' notes, and other preproduction materials to ensure the restoration is as complete as possible.

Section 2

Established in 1990 by Martin Scorsese, the Film Foundation helps to conserve motion picture history by supporting preservation and restoration projects at film archives. The foundation has helped save more than 560 motion pictures. It prioritizes funding each year according to physical urgency. Also taken into account is the significance of a project, whether the film is an important work of a writer, actor, or director, or a technical first, or whether it approaches some social issue ahead of its time.

At its core, the **Film Foundation** represents a natural progression for Scorsese, arguably the world's greatest film enthusiast. Margaret Bodde, a film producer and executive director of **the Film Foundation**, says, "With **Marty**, what is so remarkable is his dedication to preservation and film as culture and an art form. **He** doesn't do it as an obligation; **he** does it because he wants future generations to be as inspired by film as **he** was."

Scorsese's storied career gained its inspiration from the numerous films he viewed growing up in Manhattan's Little Italy. **One film** that inspired **Scorsese** with a model for how to shoot the fight sequences in his 1980 film *Raging Bull* was *The Red Shoes* (1948), the ballet-centered masterpiece created by the powerhouse British directing team of Michael Powell and Emeric Pressburger. **The Film Foundation** funded its restoration in 2006, the first fully digital restoration with which it was involved.

Working from the original film negatives, preservationists found that tiny imperfections from **the original film** development had been exacerbated by time. In addition, much of **the film** had shrunk. Colors flickered, became mottled, and showed other types of distortion. **The film** also showed red, blue, and green specks throughout. Worst of all, mold had damaged the negatives.

After **the film** underwent an extensive cleaning process, it was digitized: 579,000 individual frames had to be scanned. Colors were reregistered, scratches smoothed, flecks removed, and color inconsistencies addressed. Last, a new filmstrip was produced.

The rapid shift from photochemical to digital production has raised concerns. Bodde says, "If a film is born digital, there should be a film output" because of the possibility of data corruption or the unavailability of playback mechanisms. **The Film Foundation** is working with archivists, technologists, and preservationists to ensure that photochemical preservation continues.

The foundation also offers an interdisciplinary curriculum to help develop visual literacy and film knowledge. This curriculum, The Story of Movies, has been embraced by well over thirty thousand schools. All of this effort works to ensure that future generations know the wonder of watching Moira Shearer move through the vivid, Technicolor dreamscapes of *The Red Shoes* and many other treasures of our film heritage.

The passage can be divided into two sections. The first section is general, while the second is specific.

I. In the first part, the author describes the difficulties of preserving *film* (general). Notice the continual use of plural nouns (*films, movies, preservationists*).

II. In the second part, a specific example (Martin Scorsese and his Film Foundation) is used to support the idea that film preservation is difficult. Notice the repetition of the specific name *Martin Scorsese* and the focus on a single organization, *the Film Foundation*.

The transition occurs in the fifth paragraph because that is the place where the focus shifts from the general difficulties of film preservation to the much narrower focus on Scorsese and his foundation. Note that Martin Scorsese's name appears for the first time here, and that it is the first time in the passage that the author refers to a specific person and organization.

If you were to skim through the passage, you could use that organization to tell you where to slow down and where to speed up. For example, you should read the introduction slowly (as always) because it introduces the central problem discussed in the passage:

> The cellulose nitrate film on which movies were recorded until 1950 is <u>flammable and highly susceptible to deterioration</u>. The medium that replaced nitrate, cellulose acetate, solved the flammability problem, but is <u>vulnerable to disintegration, shrinkage, and breakage</u>.

The underlined phrases clearly indicate the point: old films are delicate and easily destroyed. With that piece of information in mind, you can reasonably assume the next few paragraphs will be related to the same idea. And sure enough, if you read only the topic sentences, you can see that that is in fact the case:

> Film needs to be stored in a temperature and moisture controlled environment.

> Actual restoration is a further, complicated step that many films will never undergo.

> The work also requires old-fashioned research.

Since you know that these sentences are simply there to support the idea that preserving film is hard, it's up to you to decide how much of each paragraph you want to read. If you want to get an idea of the details discussed in each paragraph, you are of course free to do so; however, keep in mind that you will probably still need to go back to the passage in order to answer questions that ask about those details.

If you want to glance over the body of each paragraph, looking for major transitions that may be important later on (e.g., the word *but* in the last sentence of paragraph three), you can also do so.

Or if you want to go really fast, you can simply read the topic sentences and skip everything else. Until, that is, you get to paragraph five, when things start to change:

> Established in 1990 by Martin Scorsese, the Film Foundation helps to conserve motion picture history by supporting preservation and restoration projects at film archives.

In comparison to the earlier topic sentences, which are short, direct, and to-the-point, this sentence is much longer, much more detailed, and provides much more concrete information (a name, a date, an organization). If you're only focusing on topic sentences, the difference is striking. It's also the equivalent of a flashing red signal, telling you to slow down and pay attention.

If you can recognize that the beginning of the fifth paragraph is important, it makes sense to slow down for a few sentences and find out some basic information about Scorsese's Film Foundation. Think of it as an introduction to the second half of the passage. Once you get a good sense of why the foundation is important, you can start to skim the topic sentences of the following paragraphs. Because you know that this section will focus on Scorsese's Film Foundation, you can assume that the following paragraphs will discuss some aspect of it. And indeed, that is the case for the following two paragraphs, as the topic sentences indicate:

> At its core, the Film Foundation represents a natural progression for Scorsese, arguably the world's greatest film enthusiast.

> Scorsese's storied career gained its inspiration from the numerous films he viewed growing up in Manhattan's Little Italy.

In the **third paragraph**, however, you probably want to slow down again because a new idea is introduced, and there is **another move from general to specific**. Instead of continuing to describe Scorsese and his Foundation in general, the author shifts to discussing one particular film. If you read the rest of the passage without identifying that film and its importance, your comprehension will suffer. Once you identify that information, however, you can go back to looking at topic sentences.

> After the film underwent an extensive cleaning process, it was digitized: 579,000 individual frames had to be scanned.

> The rapid shift from photochemical to digital production has raised concerns.

Then, of course, you want to read the conclusion slowly. In this case, it opens up the discussion, explaining the **larger significance** of Scorsese's Foundation: its **goal** is to ensure that future generations have access to influential classic films.

Now you have a general "map" of how the passage is divided, what each section discusses, and where the shift from section to section occurs. When questions ask you to consider specific details, the outline you've created will allow you to think logically about where they're likely to be located.

Knowing how to identify sections is also crucial to answering questions that ask about how the passages as a whole are organized. For example, a question about the organization of the passage we've been looking at might read something like this:

1. Which of the following best describes the organization of this passage?

   A. an extended comparison of the process by which digital and photochemical films are preserved.
   B. a discussion of the film preservation process followed by a description of a specific organization devoted to restoring films.
   C. a description of a film's plot followed by specific examples of the steps taken to preserve that film.
   D. an overview of the steps taken to restore a film, from initial selection through digitization.

If you've taken the time to identify the two sections as general and specific, you can jump almost immediately to (B).

5 Literal Comprehension

· ·

Literal comprehension questions make up a large percentage of the ACT Reading Test, and they come in many shapes and sizes. Some ask you to locate specific information, while others ask you to summarize the content of a passage or an idea it discusses. Still others ask you to identify what a particular word or phrase refers to.

Locating Information

Questions that ask you to identify particular pieces of information within a passage are among the most straightforward on the ACT. Indeed, the answer is typically stated word-for-word (or almost word-for-word) in the passage. So there's nothing to worry about, right? Well, not necessarily. **Although these questions appear to test nothing more than the ability to pick words out of a passage, they are also reasoning questions in disguise** – that is, they require you to use your knowledge of how passages are organized in order to think logically about where the necessary information is located.

Think of it this way: questions that ask you to identify pieces of factual information do not normally contain line references. If you don't remember the answer or where it's mentioned, you're in trouble. At this point, there are two things you must avoid: rereading the passage slowly, or leaping frantically and quasi-randomly from one section to another. Doing these things can cost you huge amounts of time and leave you behind for the entire section. If, however, you take a few extra seconds upfront to think carefully about the specific words you're looking for and where they most likely appear, you can save a lot of time.

As a general rule, you should break down literal comprehension questions as follows:

1) Identify the key word or phrase in the question and circle/underline it.

2) Think logically about where in the passage that topic is discussed.

If you have no idea, either scan topic sentences until you find one related to the word you're looking for, then read the paragraph slowly; OR pull your finger down the side of the page as you scan the passage for the key word. **If you choose this route, it is crucial that you use your finger to focus your eye.** Otherwise, you can easily overlook key information.

3) When you've found the key word, slowly read each section where it appears.

Remember that the answer will be stated literally; if the answer isn't in the section you're reading, it must be somewhere else. Try reading the surrounding sentences (before and after), and if that doesn't work, skip ahead to the next mention of the key word.

Let's look back at our example. Again, pay attention to how the passage is divided.

Section 1

A barn. A warehouse. A closet. These locations have something in common: They all contained films or parts of films that were missing and presumed lost forever. According to reliable estimates, at least 50 percent of all films made for public exhibition before 1950 have been lost. Move into the silent era, and the estimate shoots up to 90 percent. The cellulose nitrate film on which movies were recorded until 1950 is flammable and highly susceptible to deterioration. The medium that replaced nitrate, cellulose acetate, solved the flammability problem, but is vulnerable to disintegration, shrinkage, and breakage.

Film needs to be stored in a temperature and moisture controlled environment. Film archives all over the world maintain such climate-controlled storage facilities as a first line of defense. Transferring nitrate film to stable safety stock is a second precaution film preservationists take.

Actual restoration is a further, complicated step that many films will never undergo. Restoring celluloid films is a costly, time-consuming process that requires expert handling in one of the few photochemical labs that still exist; today, more films are being restored through digital correction, but this work is also labor-intensive.

The work also requires old-fashioned research. Film is an art form that everyone from producers to theater owners have felt entitled to alter to fit their requirements, including shortening films to maximize the number of screenings and cutting out material the exhibitor deemed inappropriate. Therefore, research must be done to find shooting scripts, directors' notes, and other preproduction materials to ensure the restoration is as complete as possible.

Section 2

Established in 1990 by Martin Scorsese, the Film Foundation helps to conserve motion picture history by supporting preservation and restoration projects at film archives. The foundation has helped save more than 560 motion pictures. It prioritizes funding each year according to physical urgency. Also taken into account is the significance of a project, whether the film is an important work of a writer, actor, or director, or a technical first, or whether it approaches some social issue ahead of its time.

At its core, the Film Foundation represents a natural progression for Scorsese, arguably the world's greatest film enthusiast. Margaret Bodde, a film producer and executive director of the Film Foundation, says, "With Marty, what is so remarkable is his dedication to preservation and film as culture and an art form. He doesn't do it as an obligation; he does it because he wants future generations to be as inspired by film as he was."

Scorsese's storied career gained its inspiration from the numerous films he viewed growing up in Manhattan's Little Italy. One film that inspired Scorsese with a model for how to shoot the fight sequences in his 1980 film *Raging Bull* was *The Red Shoes* (1948), the ballet-centered masterpiece created by the powerhouse British directing team of Michael Powell and Emeric Pressburger. The Film Foundation funded its restoration in 2006, the first fully digital restoration with which it was involved.

Working from the original film negatives, preservationists found that tiny imperfections from the original film development had been exacerbated by time. In addition, much of the film had shrunk. Colors flickered, became mottled, and showed other types of distortion. The film also showed red, blue, and green specks throughout. Worst of all, mold had damaged the negatives.

After the film underwent an extensive cleaning process, it was digitized: 579,000 individual frames had to be scanned. Colors were reregistered, scratches smoothed, flecks removed, and color inconsistencies addressed. Last, a new filmstrip was produced.

The rapid shift from photochemical to digital production has raised concerns. Bodde says, "If a film is born digital, there should be a film output" because of the possibility of data corruption or the unavailability of playback mechanisms. The Film Foundation is working with archivists, technologists, and preservationists to ensure that photochemical preservation continues.

The foundation also offers an interdisciplinary curriculum to help develop visual literacy and film knowledge. This curriculum, The Story of Movies, has been embraced by well over thirty thousand schools. All of this effort works to ensure that future generations know the wonder of watching Moira Shearer move through the vivid, Technicolor dreamscapes of *The Red Shoes* and many other treasures of our film heritage.

1. The passage states that film restoration requires old-fashioned research because:

   A. digital correction is a costly and time-consuming process.

   B. films are altered by everyone from producers to theater managers to fit their own needs.

   C. inappropriate material must be removed before films can be shown to viewers.

   D. a lack of climate control damages celluloid so that original images can no longer be seen.

The question asks about what the passage *states*, so we know that the wording of the answer choice won't be too far off from what's in the passage. The real question is where that information is located. Instead of just scanning the passage and hoping we stumble across it, we're going to work systematically to identify the correct information.

1) Identify the key word in the question.

The question mentions two specific ideas: "film restoration" and "old-fashioned research." **How do you decide which one to focus on? You look for the one that's more specific. That idea is more likely to appear in only one place, close to the answer, and you want to reread as little material as possible.** In this case, "film restoration" is one of the main subjects of the passage – those words are mentioned many times, so checking each instance of them could cost you a lot of time. On the other hand, "old-fashioned research" is much more specific to the question. If you focus on finding that phrase, you'll probably find the answer much more quickly.

2) Think about where the answer is likely to be located.

Consider what each section talks about: the first section discusses the general difficulties of film restoration and preservation in general, while the second section focuses on the specific role of the Film Foundation in helping to restore films. The question doesn't have anything to do with the Film Foundation, and "film restoration" is pretty general, so it seems reasonable to start by assuming that the answer is located somewhere in the first four paragraphs. If it turns out that you're wrong, you can always keep reading, but this way you'll start off with some focus.

3) Skim the first paragraph, and then read topic sentences looking for the key word.

Because it can be difficult to tell what information an introduction will include, you risk missing something important if you just read the beginning. As you scan, put your finger on the page to focus your eye and "remind" your brain that you're only looking for that specific phrase. At any rate, it's not there, so move on to topic sentences. You can also pull your finger down the rest of each paragraph, scanning it for the key word, but you must resist the urge to read closely because doing so will cost you far too much time.

Film needs to be stored in a temperature and moisture controlled environment. No.

Actual restoration is a further, complicated step that many films will never undergo. No.

The work also requires old-fashioned research. Bingo!

So now that we know where the necessary information is located, we can read the rest of the paragraph carefully.

What do we learn? That old-fashioned research is necessary because *everyone from theater owners to film producers has felt entitled to alter [films] to fit their requirements.* Which is exactly what (B) says.

Now granted, if you looked long enough, you would probably find your way to that answer on your own eventually. But the point of this little exercise isn't to see whether you can find the answer – it's to teach you to find the answer as quickly and efficiently as possible. In this case, the necessary information was buried pretty deep in the passage. If you didn't remember where it was located and went hunting through the passage at random, the whole thing might have taken you twice as long.

Same Idea, Different Words

Although many correct answers to literal comprehension questions will restate the passage verbatim, some correct answers will rephrase the wording of the passage using synonyms. In such cases, your goal is to find the answer that expresses the same *idea* expressed in the passage, not necessarily the one that uses identical *wording*. If you always expect to see the exact wording of the passage repeated, you can easily overlook or become confused by answers that paraphrase the passage. (For an *Official Guide, 2018* example, look at question #25 on p. 77. The passage refers to the _relationship_ between humans and natural forces in lines 46-47, while the correct answer, (B), refers to an "interplay.")

For instance, the question on the previous page could also be accompanied by these answers:

1. According to the passage, film restoration requires old-fashioned research because:

    A. digital correction is a costly and time-consuming process.
    B. the existing version of a film can differ substantially from the original version.
    C. inappropriate material must be removed before films can be shown to viewers.
    D. a lack of climate control damages celluloid so that original images can no longer be seen.

In this case, the idea in (B) is still correct, but it presents the information using very different words than those in the passage. If *everyone from film producers to theater managers has altered [films] to fit their requirements,* then by definition, those films differ from their original versions.

Let's try one more question:

1. The passage indicates that a difficulty involved in
    digitally restoring *The Red Shoes* was that:

    A. tiny imperfections in the original film had grown
        worse over time.
    B. Michael Powell and Emeric Pressberger did not
        support the Film Foundation's efforts.
    C. technology needed to restore the film was prone to
        malfunction.
    D. scratches and flecks made the production of a new
        film strip impossible.

Our strategy is going to be similar to that used for the previous question, but there is a shortcut you can use here – one that allows you to locate the answer very, very quickly.

1) Identify the key word/phrase.

Focus on *The Red Shoes* because it's a title and therefore must be italicized.

2) Think about where it's likely to be located.

The title must be located where the italics appear, and they only appear in two places: the seventh paragraph (lines 61-69) and the last paragraph. The information you need must be located in one of those two places. Normally the conclusion is pretty important; however, in this case, the last paragraph focuses on the Film Foundation's work in schools and doesn't discuss the actual restoration process. You should therefore start by looking in the seventh paragraph.

3) Reread carefully.

This is where you need to start paying attention. If you only read the paragraph in which the title appears, you won't find the answer. Be careful not to fall into a rereading loop and start searching for something that isn't there. Remember that if you don't see the answer to a literal comprehension question in the section you're reading, it's probably somewhere else.

If you keep going, you'll see that the answer is discussed in the following (eighth) paragraph. What makes the question potentially challenging, however, is the fact that the word *difficulty* never appears. You must infer the idea of difficulty based on the content of the paragraph (mottled colors, mold damage, etc.).

An additional challenge is that this question indirectly tests vocabulary as well. The passage states that *tiny imperfections in the original film had been <u>exacerbated</u> by time*. If you don't know what *exacerbated* (made worse) means, you can of course figure out that it's something bad based on the fact that the rest of the passage talks about the poor condition of the film; however, if you don't know the exact definition, there's a chance that you'll get nervous and second-guess yourself.

But that would be a shame because the answer is in fact (A).

Important: when correct answers rephrase information from a passage, they may contain language that is considerably more <u>neutral</u> than the language used in the passage.

For example, let's return to question #25 on p. 77 of *The Official Guide, 2018*. The language of the passage in lines 36-46 is quite dramatic (*dynamic and dangerous relationship*), but (B) removes the heightened language entirely. For that reason, (C) is an exceptionally attractive distractor. The adjectives "dynamic" and "powerful" clearly reflect the description in the passage. This answer is incorrect only because the passage focuses on fisherman rather than farmers.

Likewise, Passage B on p. 372 clearly discusses Hemingway's depiction of himself and his contemporaries in terms of positive (Hemingway) and negative (his contemporaries); however, in #26, (F), the correct answer rephrases that idea much more broadly and neutrally, referring only to "a particular portrait." In both cases, the incorrect answers are more specific and/or include words taken verbatim from the passage.

Multiple Answers

These types of questions are inevitably an annoyance because they ask you to juggle multiple pieces of information in a single answer choice. Although these questions are typically more time- consuming than those that only include one piece of information, they do not have to take up inordinate amounts of time.

The first thing to keep in mind is that all of the answers will be located in the same general area, although they may sometimes involve more than one paragraph. If you start looking all over the passage, chances are you'll miss something right under your nose.

Furthermore, you can often use the configurations of the various answer choices to eliminate multiple options quickly. It is rare that you will need to worry about the details of each answer individually.

For example:

1. The passage states that the process of digitizing *The Red Shoes* involved:

    A. reregistering colors, smoothing scratches, and old-fashioned research.
    B. reregistering colors, producing a new filmstrip, and undergoing an extensive cleaning process.
    C. addressing color inconsistencies, reregistering colors, and old-fashioned research.
    D. addressing color inconsistencies, removing scratches, and scanning each frame.

Once you've identified the section of the passage where the information is located, the fastest and simplest way to work through this type of question is to start with the first answer and check out each option individually. When you come across a piece of information that wasn't involved in digitizing *The Red Shoes*, you can then cross out every answer that mentions it. Then repeat for the remaining options. You should be left with only one possibility pretty quickly.

In this case, you can again find the necessary section easily by scanning for the italicized title *The Red Shoes*. If you start where the name appears and read down from there, you'll hit the right spot quickly.

> *After the film underwent an extensive cleaning process, it was digitized: 579,000 individual frames had to be scanned. Colors were reregistered, scratches smoothed, flecks removed, and color inconsistencies addressed. Last, a new filmstrip was produced.*

Now you can start checking each option.

(A): the paragraph mentions *reregistering colors* and *smoothing flecks and scratches*, but there's nothing about *old-fashioned research*. That eliminates both (A) and (C).

(B): you know from (A) that *reregistering colors* is there, so you only have to think about the other two parts of the answer. The passage states that *a new filmstrip was produced*, so that's fine, too. Now be careful. The question asks about the digitization process, and the passage states that the cleaning occurred *before* digitization began (yes, ACT questions do actually require that level of subtlety sometimes). So (B) doesn't actually answer the question. That leaves (D).

Other multiple-answer questions are presented in Roman numeral format. In some cases, you will be able to use the configuration of the answer choices to eliminate multiple answers simultaneously. At other times, however, you may need to check every option individually. As you consider each possibility, you should keep in mind that incorrect answers may still be mentioned in the passage – they just won't answer the question correctly.

> **2.** The passage indicates that celluloid film restoration requires:
>
>   I.   expert handling
>   II. old-fashioned research
>   III. digital correction

The first thing to do is to find the necessary section of the passage – in a passage this dense, you should not try to rely on your memory. The question asks about "celluloid film restoration" in general, rather than the restoration of a specific film, suggesting that you need to look at the first part of the passage. Sure enough, if you start scanning topic sentences from the beginning, you'll find what you need in only the third paragraph. But be careful! The discussion continues into the fourth paragraph; if you stop at the end of the third paragraph, you'll miss key information.

Remember also to keep in mind exactly what the question says – it asks specifically what celluloid film restoration "requires", not what it "can involve." That's a subtle distinction, but it's an important one.

> *Actual restoration is a further, complicated step that many films will never undergo. Restoring celluloid films is a costly, time-consuming process that <u>requires expert handling</u> in one of the few photochemical labs that still exist; today, more films are being restored through digital correction, but this work is also labor-intensive.*

The work also <u>requires old-fashioned research</u>. Film is an art form that everyone from producers to theater owners have felt entitled to alter to fit their requirements, including shortening films to maximize the number of screenings and cutting out material the exhibitor deemed inappropriate. Therefore, research must be done to find shooting scripts, directors' notes, and other preproduction materials to ensure the restoration is as complete as possible.

Now look at the answers:

F. I only
G. I and II only
H. II and III only
J. I, II, and III

The passage states that *expert handling* is required, so we know that I is correct. Eliminate (H).

II: The beginning of the fourth paragraph states clearly that *The work also requires old fashioned research*, so II must be correct as well. Eliminate (F).

III: Be careful. The passage states that *today, more films are being restored through digital correction*, but it does not say that digital correction is **required** to restore celluloid film. Eliminate (J).

That leaves you with (G), which is correct.

Alternately, you could read the paragraphs in question straight through, putting a check mark next to each correct answer. You would end up with I and II, again making (G) the answer.

If the answers were arranged this way, the process could go faster.

2. The passage indicates that celluloid film restoration requires:

I. expert handling
II. digital correction
III. old-fashioned research

F. I only
G. I and III only
H. II and III only
J. I, II, and III

In this case, you could cross off both (H) and (J) immediately, once you realized that II was incorrect. Instead of checking out three separate answers, you would only have to check two. If you stopped before the first line of the fourth paragraph, however, you could easily overlook the fact that celluloid restoration involves old-fashioned research and pick (F).

EXCEPT and NOT Questions

"All of the following EXCEPT" and "Which of the following is NOT?" questions are based on the same principle as multiple-answer questions. The primary difference is that they ask you to juggle four pieces of information rather than three. As is true for multiple-answer questions, the incorrect piece of information may either not be mentioned at all, or it may be mentioned in a different context.

Important: Always underline or circle the word EXCEPT or NOT. Otherwise, you risk losing track of the question and doing exactly the opposite of what it asks.

For example:

1. All of the following are mentioned in the passage as
    factors that the Film Foundation takes into account
    when prioritizing funding for restoring films **<u>EXCEPT</u>**:

    A. physical urgency.
    B. commercial success.
    C. technical innovation.
    D. consideration of social issues.

The question asks about the Film Foundation, so the answer must be located in the second half of the passage. The end focuses on the restoration of *The Red Shoes*, so you can assume that the correct answer will appear closer to the middle. Sure enough, the key phrase is located in line 46.

> *Established in 1990 by Martin Scorsese, the Film Foundation helps to conserve motion picture history by supporting preservation and restoration projects at film archives. The foundation... <u>prioritizes funding</u> each year according to <u>physical urgency</u>. Also taken into account is the significance of a project, whether the film <u>is an important work of a writer, actor, or director, or a technical first</u>, or <u>whether it approaches some social issue ahead of its time</u>.*

As you locate each piece of information in the passage, cross off the entire answer choice. Eliminating as you read will reduce the amount of information you need to keep in your head at once time and prevent you from becoming confused about what you are looking for.

To reiterate: you are looking for the factor that the passage does NOT mention. If an answer choice IS mentioned in the passage, it is wrong.

Remember also that information from the passage may be repeated verbatim in the answers, or it may be rephrased slightly.

So now, what factors **does** the Film Foundation take into account when prioritizing funding?

*   *physical urgency.* Eliminate (A).

    A. ~~physical urgency.~~
    B. commercial success.
    C. technical innovation.
    D. consideration of social issues.

- *whether the film is…a technical first* (=technical innovation). Eliminate (C).

  A. ~~physical urgency.~~
  B. commercial success.
  C. ~~technical innovation.~~
  D. consideration of social issues.

- *whether it approaches some social issue ahead of its time* (=consideration of social issues). Eliminate (D).

  A. ~~physical urgency.~~
  B. commercial success.
  C. ~~technical innovation.~~
  D. ~~consideration of social issues.~~

The passage says nothing about whether a film's commercial success affects the Film Foundation's decision to fund its restoration. So (B) is NOT in the passage, making that answer correct.

Order of Events

This type of question requires you to identify where, in a series of events, a particular event occurred (e.g., first, last), or to put a series of events in order from first to last. The primary challenge is that the events will not be discussed in chronological order in the passage, and you must use information from different sections of the passage to determine the sequence in which the events occurred.

The "Film Foundation" passage is printed again on the following page so that you do not have to flip back to reread it. You will need to refer to it for the question that appears afterward.

A barn. A warehouse. A closet. These locations have something in common: They all contained films or parts of films that were missing and presumed lost forever. According to reliable estimates, at least 50 percent of all films made for public exhibition before 1950 have been lost. Move into the silent era, and the estimate shoots up to 90 percent. The cellulose nitrate film on which movies were recorded until 1950 is flammable and highly susceptible to deterioration. The medium that replaced nitrate, cellulose acetate, solved the flammability problem, but is vulnerable to disintegration, shrinkage, and breakage.

Film needs to be stored in a temperature and moisture controlled environment. Film archives all over the world maintain such climate-controlled storage facilities as a first line of defense. Transferring nitrate film to stable safety stock is a second precaution film preservationists take.

Actual restoration is a further, complicated step that many films will never undergo. Restoring celluloid films is a costly, time-consuming process that requires expert handling in one of the few photochemical labs that still exist; today, more films are being restored through digital correction, but this work is also labor-intensive.

The work also requires old-fashioned research. Film is an art form that everyone from producers to theater owners has felt entitled to alter to fit their requirements, including shortening films to maximize the number of screenings and cutting out material the exhibitor deemed inappropriate. Therefore, research must be done to find shooting scripts, directors' notes, and other preproduction materials to ensure the restoration is as complete as possible.

Established in 1990 by Martin Scorsese, the Film Foundation helps to conserve motion picture history by supporting preservation and restoration projects at film archives. The foundation has helped save more than 560 motion pictures. It prioritizes funding each year according to physical urgency. Also taken into account is the significance of a project, whether the film is an important work of a writer, actor, or director, or a technical first, or whether it approaches some social issue ahead of its time.

At its core, the Film Foundation represents a natural progression for Scorsese, arguably the world's greatest film enthusiast. Margaret Bodde, a film producer and executive director of the Film Foundation, says, "With Marty, what is so remarkable is his dedication to preservation and film as culture and an art form. He doesn't do it as an obligation; he does it because he wants future generations to be as inspired by film as he was."

Scorsese's storied career gained its inspiration from the numerous films he viewed growing up in Manhattan's Little Italy. One film that inspired Scorsese with a model for how to shoot the fight sequences in his 1980 film *Raging Bull* was *The Red Shoes* (1948), the ballet-centered masterpiece created by the powerhouse British directing team of Michael Powell and Emeric Pressburger. The Film Foundation funded its restoration in 2006, the first fully digital restoration with which it was involved.

Working from the original film negatives, preservationists found that tiny imperfections from the original film development had been exacerbated by time. In addition, much of the film had shrunk. Colors flickered, became mottled, and showed other types of distortion. The film also showed red, blue, and green specks throughout. Worst of all, mold had damaged the negatives.

After the film underwent an extensive cleaning process, it was digitized: 579,000 individual frames had to be scanned. Colors were reregistered, scratches smoothed, flecks removed, and color inconsistencies addressed. Last, a new filmstrip was produced.

The rapid shift from photochemical to digital production has raised concerns. Bodde says, "If a film is born digital, there should be a film output" because of the possibility of data corruption or the unavailability of playback mechanisms. The Film Foundation is working with archivists, technologists, and preservationists to ensure that photochemical preservation continues.

The foundation also offers an interdisciplinary curriculum to help develop visual literacy and film knowledge. This curriculum, The Story of Movies, has been embraced by well over thirty thousand schools. All of this effort works to ensure that future generations know the wonder of watching Moira Shearer move through the vivid, Technicolor dreamscapes of *The Red Shoes* and many other treasures of our film heritage.

1. Based on the passage, which of the following occurred first chronologically?

    A. the restoration of *The Red Shoes*.
    B. the making of *Raging Bull*.
    C. the Film Foundation's establishment.
    D. the use of cellulose acetate to record films.

Unfortunately, there's no consistent shortcut for this type of question, but if you use your general knowledge of the passage, you can eliminate some answers without having to reread anything. For example, if you remember that the passage discusses *The Red Shoes* as an example of a film restored by the Film Foundation, you can make the logical assumption that the Film Foundation was established **before** *The Red Shoes* was restored. That means (A) can't have occurred first.

If you'd rather just start by checking out each answer in the passage, you can do that as well.

(A): As discussed earlier, the words *The Red Shoes* are easy to find because they are italicized. Now be careful. The passage indicates the film was *made* in 1948, but that it was *restored* in 2006.

(B): The words *Raging Bull* are easy to find; aside from *The Red Shoes*, they're the only italicized words in the passage. The film was made in 1980, which came before 2006, so (A) is out.

(C): The date of the Film Foundation's establishment is easy to find as well. It's mentioned at the start of the discussion about that organization, in line 35. The passage states that the organization was founded in 1990, which obviously came after 1980, so (C) is out.

(D): Even though cellulose acetate is mentioned in the last answer choice, it's mentioned *first* in the passage. It's also the sort of picky little detail you're unlikely to remember, and unfortunately, there's nothing to indicate where it's mentioned. In this case, though, you'll find it quickly if you start scanning from the beginning of the passage. (Just remember to use your finger to focus your eye.) The passage states that cellulose nitrate was used until 1950, at which point it was replaced by cellulose acetate. 1950 came before 1980, so (B) is out, leaving (D) as the correct answer.

Note that if you had simply looked through the passage for the earliest date (1948), you would have gotten the question wrong. While that strategy may work for some chronology questions, it is by no means reliable; these questions are usually designed to make you do some work.

The question also could have been presented this way:

1. Which choice correctly states the order in which the following events occurred?

    A. the restoration of *The Red Shoes*, the making of *Raging Bull*, the creation of the Film Foundation, the use of cellulose acetate to record film.
    B. the use of cellulose acetate to record film, the making of *Raging Bull*, the creation of the Film Foundation, the restoration of *The Red Shoes*.
    C. the use of cellulose acetate to record film, the restoration of *The Red Shoes*, the creation of the Film Foundation, the making of *Raging Bull*.
    D. the making of *Raging Bull*, the creation of the Film Foundation, the use of cellulose acetate to record film, the restoration of *The Red Shoes*.

This question might look at lot more complicated than the previous one, but don't be fooled! You can simplify it by focusing on the first event – now you're dealing with three options instead of 16! If you check the first event in each answer, you'll see that the use of cellulose acetate occurred earliest, eliminating (A) and (D). Now look at (B) and (C); the answer that lists the second event correctly must be right by default. *Raging Bull* was made before *The Red Shoes* was restored, so (B) is correct.

Deleting Information

"Delete" questions ask you to identify what information would (primarily) be lost if a particular paragraph or section of a passage were deleted. Although they are far more common on the English Test, they do appear on the Reading Test from time to time. Do not, however, be fooled by the way these questions are phrased. In reality, asking what a passage would lose with the elimination of a given section is really just a more complicated way of asking what information is contained in that section, or what the primary focus of that information is. To make things easier for yourself, you should immediately rephrase any "Delete" question as "What is the topic of this paragraph or section?" That's much easier to wrap your head around.

For example, a "Delete" question about the "Film Foundation" passage on p. 48 could read as follows:

1. If the author were to delete the final paragraph, the passage would lose a discussion of:

    A. the Film Foundation's educational mission.
    B. how *The Red Shoes'* vivid Technicolor landscape was created.
    C. the importance of visual and film literacy in American culture.
    D. the Film Foundation's impact on previous generations.

Assuming for a moment that you don't spot the answer immediately, the easiest way to approach this question is to simply go back to the passage and briefly recap for yourself what it discusses. You might say something like, "Film Foundation goes into schools to teach about film."

(A) sums up that idea, just using slightly different words (teach + schools = education). In contrast, the incorrect answers take words included in the passage and "twist" them so that they do not accurately reflect the meaning of the passage.

Paraphrasing and Referents

The second major type of literal comprehension question is not concerned so much with your ability to locate specific facts within large swaths of information as it is with your ability to understand the literal meaning of complex constructions, and to "track" words and ideas throughout a passage. Unlike information-location questions, which generally involve straightforward language and are difficult primarily because of the time constraints involved, this question type directly tests your comprehension of sophisticated sentence structure and abstract or academic vocabulary.

On the upside, these questions usually *do* contain line references, so you don't have to worry about spending time finding information, only understanding its literal meaning. If you are a strong reader, you can most likely answer these questions fairly quickly. When they appear, you should therefore try to answer them before turning to more time-consuming items.

There are two primary types of questions in this group:

1) Paraphrasing and Summarizing

These questions ask you to rephrase, in simplified form, phrases, sentences, or paragraphs – often ones that contain challenging vocabulary or metaphorical language. Some questions explicitly ask you to identify which answer choice best paraphrases the content of the sentence, while others ask you to identify which choice best captures what an author means by a particular statement or expression. Sometimes you will be able to use contextual information to figure out the approximate meaning, even if you do not understand every single word, but other times you will have to depend primarily on the sentence itself.

2) Identifying Referents

This question type does not appear very often, but it can catch you off guard if you are not prepared for it. As discussed earlier, a person or thing can be referred to by a proper name (*William Shakespeare, Romeo and Juliet*), a pronoun (*he, it*), or another noun or phrase (*the playwright/the Bard of Avon, the play*). This question type directly tests your ability to connect those words and phrases – known as **referents** – back to the nouns to which they refer. This is a crucial skill for college-level reading: authors frequently refer to people/ideas/events in a variety of ways, and it is up to you to recognize that multiple words and phrases can refer to the same thing.

On the next page, we're going to look at some examples of these two question types. If you want, you can try them on your own before looking at the explanations beginning on the following page. Alternately, you can jump right to the explanations and use them to work through the questions.

One of the little-known turning points in the history of American travel occurred in the spring of 1869, when a handsome young preacher from Boston named William H. Murray published one of the first guidebooks to a wilderness area. In describing the Adirondack Mountains—a 9,000-square-mile expanse of lakes, forests and rivers in upstate New York—Murray broached the then-outrageous idea that an excursion into raw nature could actually be pleasurable. Before that date, most Americans considered the country's primeval landscapes only as obstacles to be conquered. But Murray's self-help opus, *Adventures in the Wilderness*, suggested that hiking, canoeing and fishing in unsullied nature were the ultimate health tonic for harried city dwellers whose constitutions were weakened by the demands of civilized life.

This radical notion had gained currency among Europeans since the Romantic age, but America was still building its leisured classes and the idea had not yet caught on with the general public. In 1869, after the horrors of the Civil War and amid the country's rapid industrialization, Murray's book became a surprise best seller. Readers were enthralled by his vision of a pure, Edenic world in the Adirondacks, where hundreds of forest-swathed lakes were gleaming "like gems...amid the folds of emerald-covered velvet." Murray argued that American cities were disease-ridden and filled with pressures that created "an intense, unnatural and often fatal tension" in their unhappy denizens. The wilderness, by contrast, restored both the spirit and body. "No axe has sounded along its mountain-sides, or echoed across its peaceful waters," Murray enthused, so "the spruce, hemlock, balsam and pine...yield upon the air, and especially at night, all their curative qualities." What's more, Murray pointed out, a new train line that had opened the year before meant that this magical world was only 36 hours' travel from New York City or Boston. The vision struck a deep chord, and his book ran into ten editions within four months.

1. Which of the following statements best paraphrases the information in the last sentence of the first paragraph (lines 11-15)?

    A. Because of *Adventures in the Wilderness*, Americans began to see the importance of preserving the natural world.
    B. After the publication of *Adventures in the Wilderness*, most Americans participated in hiking, canoeing, and fishing.
    C. *Adventures in the Wilderness* promoted the view that city dwellers could improve their health by participating in outdoor activities.
    D. As a result of *Adventures in the Wilderness*, Americans came to see nature as a force that weakened the demands of civilized life.

2. In line 30, the word *its* refers to:

    F. "an intense, unnatural, and fatal tension" (lines 26-27)
    G. "The wilderness" (line 28)
    H. "the spirit" (lines 28-29)
    J. "No axe" (line 29)

3. When the author states that the vision "struck a deep chord" (line 36), he means that it:

    A. was extremely appealing.
    B. contained musical aspects.
    C. created a physical sensation.
    D. was somewhat disturbing.

Question #1:

As a general rule, you should break "paraphrase" questions into the following steps:

1) Restate the sentence in your own words.

If you have even an approximate idea of what information you're looking for, the correct answer will be much easier to spot.

> *But Murray's self-help opus, Adventures in the Wilderness, suggested that hiking, canoeing and fishing in unsullied nature were the ultimate health tonic for harried city dwellers whose constitutions were weakened by the demands of civilized life.*

In this case, you could say something like "*Adventures in the Wilderness* suggested that hiking, canoeing, and fishing would help people who lived in cities improve their health." Which answer comes closest to expressing that idea? (C), which is correct.

Admittedly, though, the sentence cited above is fairly complex, with a lot of challenging vocabulary. If you're not accustomed to working with sentences like this, you might have difficulty understanding just what it's saying. If you feel like you get the gist, though, and don't want to waste time trying to use your own words, you can probably jump right to the answers. If your comprehension is generally pretty strong, you'll probably be able to recognize the right one. But if you still feel lost…

2) Cross out confusing information.

If you simply read the sentence without the confusing parts, you'll end up with a much clearer of what it's saying. The key is not to get distracted by what you don't know.

> *But Murray's ~~self-help opus~~, Adventures in the Wilderness, suggested that hiking, canoeing and fishing in ~~unsullied~~ nature were the ultimate health ~~tonic~~ for ~~harried~~ city dwellers ~~whose constitutions were weakened by the demands of civilized life~~.*

So basically, *Adventures in the Wilderness* said that hiking, canoeing, and fishing were good for people's health. Which again is pretty much exactly what (C) says. It just replaces the specific word *sports* with the more general "outdoor activities."

It is important that you go through the process of trying to understand – and simplify – the sentence on your own before you look at the answers. Otherwise, you can easily be fooled by answers that sound plausible but are completely wrong. (A), for instance, sounds just like the sort of answer the ACT would like: it talks about preserving the environment, which is always a good thing in the ACT's playbook. The problem, however, is that this answer is totally unconnected to the passage.

(B) is also easy to fall for if you forget that the question is asking you to *paraphrase* the sentence. While many correct answers include short word-for-word sections of the passage, answers that use **long** sections verbatim from the passage tend to be incorrect. (B), for instance, takes the literal wording of the passage and rewrites it from the wrong angle – the passage says nothing about "most Americans" taking up hiking, canoeing, and fishing as a result of Murray's book. (D) plays a similar trick – it quotes the passage verbatim but distorts the words completely. The passage states that *city dwellers…were weakened by the demands of civilized life*, whereas the answer indicates that "<u>nature</u> weakened civilized life."

If you're still stuck, you can also:

3) Consider the context.

Reading a sentence or two before and after the line reference will generally help you gain a better understanding of the phrase or sentence in question. It will not, however, always give you sufficient information to answer the question.

For example, the sentence in line 11 includes the word *but*, indicating that it will present a contrast to the previous sentence. What does the previous sentence tell us? That before Murray's book appeared, most Americans viewed primeval landscapes (nature) *as obstacles to be conquered*. So logically, the sentence begun by *but* must express the opposite idea – something along the idea that Americans began to have a more positive, harmonious view of nature. Unfortunately, that doesn't get you terribly far in this case. You might be able to eliminate (D), which doesn't make much sense, but you still need to consider the other answers.

Question #2:

Answering pronoun-referent questions such as this is primarily a matter of logic – if you cannot identify the correct noun when you reread the necessary part of the passage, plug each answer into the passage in place of the pronoun and see whether it makes sense.

> *Murray argued that American cities were disease-ridden and filled with pressures that created "an intense, unnatural and often fatal tension" in their unhappy denizens. The wilderness, by contrast, restored both the spirit and body. "No axe has sounded along its mountainsides, or echoed across its peaceful waters," Murray enthused, so "the spruce, hemlock, balsam and pine...yield upon the air, and especially at night, all their curative qualities."*

(F): "No axe has sounded along an intense, unnatural, and fatal tension's mountainsides… "

Absolutely not. This makes no sense whatsoever.

(G): "No axe has sounded along the wilderness's mountainsides…."

That works. Wilderness does generally contain mountainsides.

(H): "No axe has sounded along the spirit's mountainsides…"

No. Spirits don't have mountainsides.

(J): "No axe has sounded along the axe's mountainsides…"

No. Axes don't have mountainsides either.

So (G) is the only possibility. And when you think about it in context, it makes sense: the passage, after all, is about the wilderness.

Question #3

The phrase *struck a deep chord* is explained for you immediately after it is mentioned: the passage states that the book *ran into ten editions within four months*, indicating that it was extremely popular. Logically, then, the phrase must mean something very positive, such as "had a big effect on" or "was really liked by." (A) is the most consistent with that idea.

Literal vs. Figurative

Some literal vs. figurative questions are basically vocabulary-in-context questions in reverse. Instead of taking a single word from the passage that is used figuratively or in its second meaning, and asking you to identify its literal/most common meaning, these questions ask you to identify which of four words from the passage is used figuratively.

Other literal vs. figurative questions ask you to identify whether a word or phrase should be understood literally or figuratively. **Although there are exceptions, you can generally start with the assumption that "literal" answers are likely to be incorrect.** If the ACT goes out of its way to ask whether a particular statement should be taken literally, chances are it shouldn't.

One of the little-known turning points in the history of American travel occurred in the spring of 1869, when a handsome young preacher from Boston named William H. H. Murray published one of the first guidebooks to a
5 wilderness area. In describing the Adirondack Mountains —a 9,000-square-mile expanse of lakes, forests and rivers in upstate New York—Murray broached the then-outrageous idea that an excursion into raw nature could actually be pleasurable. Before that date, most Americans
10 considered the country's primeval landscapes only as obstacles to be conquered. But Murray's self-help opus, *Adventures in the Wilderness* suggested that hiking, canoeing and fishing in unsullied nature were the ultimate health tonic for harried city dwellers whose constitutions
15 were weakened by the demands of civilized life.

This radical notion had gained currency among Europeans since the Romantic age, but America was still building its leisured classes and the idea had not yet caught on with the general public. In 1869, after the horr-
20 ors of the Civil War and amid the country's rapid industrialization, Murray's book became a surprise best seller. Readers were enthralled by his vision of a pure, Edenic world in the Adirondacks, where hundreds of forest-swathed lakes were gleaming "like gems...amid the
25 folds of emerald-colored velvet." Murray argued that American cities were disease-ridden and filled with pressures that created "an intense, unnatural and often fatal tension" in their unhappy denizens. The wilderness, by contrast, restored both the spirit and body. "No axe has
30 sounded along its mountainsides, or echoed across its peaceful waters," Murray enthused, so "the spruce, hemlock, balsam and pine...yield upon the air, and especially at night, all their curative qualities." What's

more, Murray pointed out, a new train line that had opened
35 the year before meant this magical world was only 36 hours' travel from New York City or Boston. The vision struck a deep chord, and his book ran into ten editions within four months.

1. Which of the following words is used figuratively rather than literally?

    A. "raw" (line 8)
    B. "conquered" (line 11)
    C. "pure" (line 22)
    D. "restored" (line 29)

2. The statement that Murray's vision "struck a deep chord" (line 37) is intended to be understood:

    F. literally, because the author wants to evoke the noise of an industrialized city.
    G. literally, because the passage suggests that the wilderness was filled with echoes.
    H. figuratively, because the author is describing an emotional reaction had by readers of Murray's book.
    J. figuratively, because the passage indicates that the Adirondacks were silent.

Unfortunately, there is no real "trick" to questions such as #1; however, if you spot a word among the answer choices that has a common second meaning, it's a good idea to check it first. Otherwise, you should simply check each option in turn and consider whether it is used literally. In this case, (A) is correct because *raw* literally means "uncooked." Here, however, it is used to mean "untamed."

For #2, it's certainly helpful to be familiar with the phrase *strike a chord* – it's an expression meaning "have an (emotional) impact," e.g., *The film was successful because it struck a chord with so many viewers.* You don't even need to check the passage to identify (H) as the answer.

If you're not sure of the answer from the phrase itself, though, you should consider the context. The second half of the sentence in which the phrase appears indicates that the book *ran into ten editions within four months.* In other words, it was really popular. Why would a book about a "magical world" be so popular? Probably because it had a strong effect on a lot of people. That's just enough information to get you to (H).

Facts vs. Opinions

Fact vs. opinion questions do not appear often, but they do show up from time to time. They test your ability to recognize whether a particular statement is an objective fact or an expression of opinion – that is, a value judgment open to argument. While that might sound like an obvious distinction, it is not always so clear-cut. Authors can at times present their beliefs as objective reality rather than simply opinions. Usually, they accomplish this either by employing the sort of detached, neutral language typically associated with factual statements, or by using very strong language intended to persuade the reader that their beliefs represent the truth. For example, compare the following two statements:

Statement 1:   The Statue of Liberty's torch-bearing arm was displayed at the Centennial Exposition in Philadelphia, in 1876, and in New York from 1876 to 1882.

Statement 2:   The State of Liberty is without a doubt the most important landmark in New York City.

Statement #1 describes a documented, non-debatable historical fact. Without rock-solid new evidence, no one could argue that the Statue of Liberty's arm was actually displayed at the Centennial Exposition in Cincinnati, or that it was exhibited in New York until 1875.

Statement #2, on the other hand, expresses an opinion. The fact that the author uses very strong language (*without a doubt, most important*) and is apparently convinced that the statement is true does not make the statement objectively true. Anyone could come along and find dozens of reasons to support the idea that, say, the Empire State Building is a more important landmark. There would be no way to settle the argument definitively.

Fact vs. opinion questions tend to play by the same rules as literal vs. figurative questions. If you encounter one of these questions, you should start by assuming the statement is most likely an opinion and focus on the answer choices that say so. If the ACT bothers to ask whether a clear, strongly worded statement is actually a fact, it probably isn't. Call it a trick, but the ACT is making an important point: don't assume that a piece of information is an established fact just because an author seems convinced that it's true.

6 The Big Picture

Questions that ask about the main point or purpose/function of a passage are among the most common types of Reading questions, accompanying every type of passage and often appearing multiple times per test. These questions can be asked either about a single paragraph or the entire passage, but both types require you to distinguish between main ideas and supporting details.

Questions asking about the primary purpose or point of an entire passage appear as the first question in a set, while questions asking about specific paragraphs can appear anywhere in a set. If you have a tendency to lose sight of the big picture and are concerned about having to answer a question about the entire passage first, you should quickly check whether the first question is a primary purpose question. If it is, then you can pay particular attention to that aspect of the passage as you read. If it is not, you can safely focus on the details.

Although the main point and the primary purpose are similar, they are not precisely the same thing, and it is important to understand the difference between them so that you know what to expect when you look at the answer choices. We're going to break each type down so that you can see what it's really asking and how you can most effectively approach it.

What's the Big Idea?

Many people find main idea questions intimidating because they require a leap from the string of individual words on the page to a more general type of understanding. While there are no surefire tricks for these questions, there are some steps you can take to simplify them. **The most important thing to remember is that you do not need to spend time rereading huge amounts of text.** Occasionally, you will have to read most of a paragraph to answer a paragraph-function question, but you should never try to reread an entire passage. If you find it consistently necessary to do so (even after working through this chapter), you are better off planning to guess on big-picture questions so that you do not waste too much time.

As is true for many types of Reading questions, quickly stating and jotting down an answer in your own words before you look at the choices can be a very effective technique for recognizing correct answers to big-picture questions. You should spend no more than a few seconds and limit yourself to about five words, symbols, or abbreviations. Otherwise, you'll likely overcomplicate things and lose too much time. The goal is clarity, not eloquence, and the only person who needs to be able to read your handwriting is you.

On the other hand, if you have trouble putting the point in your own words but understand it well enough to identify it from among the answer choices, you should not waste time writing just for the sake of doing so. And if you are genuinely uncertain about the point, you are better off jumping to the answers and working by process of elimination.

If you do attempt to write the point on your own even occasionally, however, you must understand just what a main idea or point is – and what it isn't. Otherwise, stating the point in your own words won't get you very far.

Let's start with what a main point isn't:

- It is not a **topic** such as "recycling" or "modern architecture" or "the Great Depression."

- It is not a **theme** such as "oppression" or "overcoming."

A main point is the primary idea or argument that a paragraph or passage contains. It answers the question "So what?" In short, why does the author care about the topic, and what is the central idea that he or she wants to convey about it?

For example, in the "Winslow Homer" passage on p. 76 of the *Official Guide, 2018*, the **topic** of the passage is Homer's painting, and the **theme** of the passage could be described as something like "ocean and art" or "impact of ocean on Homer's art." Neither of those things, however, indicates the *effect* of the ocean on Homer's art. They do not answer the question "so what?"

The **main idea**, on the other hand, is that Homer's paintings embodied the ocean's power. More precisely, they convey the idea that the ocean and the natural world are *powers and presences that can be enjoyed and whose threats can sometimes be overcome*. Or, in super-condensed terms: WH art = power/ocean.

Finding the Point

When the main idea is directly stated in the passage, it tends to appear in a couple of specific places: most frequently at the **end of the conclusion**, although sometimes the author will be kind enough to state it somewhere in the **introduction**, usually toward the end. (Remember that while the introduction will usually be limited to the first paragraph, it may occasionally consist of the first two or even three paragraphs.) Sometimes, it may even appear in both places, as in the "Winslow Homer" passage.

As mentioned earlier, the purpose of the introduction is to present the key idea or question the passage will discuss, while the purpose of the conclusion is to reemphasize that idea for the reader. If you begin to lose focus at any point, it can be helpful to (re)read the last sentence or last few sentences.

In cases in which the point is not clearly stated at either the beginning or the end, you should look for clues indicating that the author is presenting important information or mentioning a key idea. For example, consider the Humanities passage on p. 512 of *The Official Guide*. Lines 20-21 are written entirely in capital letters, providing an immediate visual clue to their importance. Sure enough, the paragraph just below essentially states the point of the passage: after some initial difficulties, the book came to play an important role in the author's life. That information gives you the answer to #24. The author's statement that she didn't come to like the book *right away* is rephrased in (F) as "daunting at first." Far from having to consider the entire passage to answer that seemingly broad question, you can obtain all the necessary information from just one key sentence.

When you encounter questions asking you to identify the main point of a paragraph, you should also start by focusing on the beginning and end of the paragraph because main ideas are again most likely to be found in those places. If you are still not sure where a paragraph is headed after a few sentences, or feel that you are starting to become lost or confused, you can try jumping ahead to the end of the paragraph to reorient yourself.

Sometimes the author will state the main idea very directly, in which case you should mark it clearly (put a big star or write MP next to it) and move on. There is no reason to spend time rewriting the point in your own words when the author has already spelled it out, unless you feel you need the extra mental reinforcement. For example, look again at the "Winslow Homer" passage on p. 76 of *The Official Guide, 2018*. Lines 3-7 ("Through... overcome.") and 85-86 ("They...ocean.") both sum up the point clearly and directly. If you wanted to condense those lines further, you could of course write "WH paintings = power/ ocean," but otherwise, you could simply bracket those lines.

Other times, however, the author will present ideas in a subtler, more roundabout manner, and you will have to put the pieces together yourself. For example, consider the "Film Foundation" passage discussed earlier in this chapter. We can take the key information discussed in each section and put it together to get the point. Section 1 tells us that restoring film is difficult, and Section 2 tells us that Scorsese's Film Foundation is taking on that challenge. If we wanted to combine those two ideas into a single statement, we could say something like "film pres. hard BUT FF does" (Film preservation is hard, but the Film Foundation does it), or "FF pres. film = hard."

Likewise, look at the Social Science passage on p. 510 of *The Official Guide, 2018*. The first 79 lines of the passage are devoted to describing the numerous ways in which sprawl hurts cities, while the last 12 lines (the conclusion) focus on describing a potential solution to the problem – namely, that sprawl can be combatted with sensible planning policies. In order to write a main point that encompasses the entire passage, it is necessary to combine both sections into a single statement, e.g., "Sprawl BAD, good regs. help" (Sprawl is bad, but good regulations can help).

Regardless of how clearly the author spells out the point, you should use the key words and punctuation listed in the chart on p. 25 to help you identify important information. Even if authors do not spell the point out, they will almost certainly go out of their way to tell you what to pay attention to.

For Humanities or Social Science passages, the main point will generally be a relatively straightforward explanation of an event, project, or individual's importance. For personal narratives (Prose Fiction and Humanities), it will usually relate to the insight or goal a person drew from a given experience. For Natural Science passages, the main point will often relate to a new discovery or to new research that is challenging a previously accepted theory.

Determining the main point for Prose Fiction passages is often a less straightforward matter because these passages focus not on arguments but on characters' actions, reactions, and interactions. As a result, it can be helpful to think of the "point" as a very, very short summary of the central action, relationship, or problem the passage describes. If you're not sure where to look for key information, you should **focus on the conclusion** because that is where the author is most likely to indicate the significance of the action in the rest of the passage.

The passage on p. 72 of *The Official Guide, 2018* provides an excellent example of this structure. The majority of the passage focuses on the story of how the narrator received her name. Only in the last few paragraphs, and most directly in the last paragraph, does she step back and comment on the significance of the story: her father liked to "embellish," and she in turn came to prefer the factual reality emphasized in school. As a main point, you could write something like "Dad embellishes stories," or, if you're in a more poetic mood, "Dad tells tall tales."

Likewise, consider the passage on p. 510 of *The Official Guide, 2018*. It's less straightforward than the passage on p. 72, but the last few paragraphs still convey the larger idea suggested by the description that precedes them: listening to Alvin's music is a profoundly moving experience, one that transports his entire audience and commands a deep respect from them.

Recognizing Correct and Incorrect Answers

Both correct and incorrect answers to main-idea questions tend to follow some general patterns. Although there are many exceptions, these patterns can be helpful to keep in mind when you are initially uncertain about what you are looking for. While they offer no guarantee, they do provide a way of "bootstrapping" your way into the answer, allowing you to make educated guesses even when you do not see a clear relationship between the wording of the answer choice and the passage.

First, because main-idea questions ask about the passage in general, correct answers are more likely to be phrased in a neutral or "vague" manner. For example, they may refer to "a certain individual" rather than state that individual's name. Incorrect answers, on the other hand, tend to refer to details from the passage. The more specific the information a given answer choice contains, the more likely that information will *not* apply to the entire passage.

Correct answers also tend to be worded moderately, whereas incorrect answers are more likely to include "extreme" language such as *always, (n)ever, fundamentally,* and *most*. In addition, you should be suspicious of answers that include specific words/phrases from the passage, especially challenging vocabulary words that many test-takers are unlikely to know (e.g., *dour*). Main-idea questions are not simply testing your ability to recognize words from the passage but to make a leap from concrete to abstract. As a result, answers that quote the passage verbatim are more likely to be *incorrect*.

Using the Point to Answer Other Questions

Identifying the point isn't important only for questions that explicitly ask about it. In fact, keeping the point in mind can help you answer questions that at first glance seem unrelated to it. Using the point this way is one of the most effective strategies for cutting down on time. Instead of having to hunt through the passage, you can sometimes jump to the answer in a matter of seconds. To be sure, ACT passages and questions can be unpredictable, so this technique does have its limits. Knowing the point won't get you very far when you're dealing with a set of mostly detail-based questions. But on many other question sets, thinking about the point as you work through the questions will help you often enough that it is well worth your while to sum it up and write it down, regardless of whether there are any questions that explicitly ask about it.

For example, consider the Social Science passage on p. 510 of *The Official Guide, 2018*. It provides a stellar example of an author who goes out of his way to announce the key ideas. If you're actively looking for the clues, there's almost no way to miss them. Highly charged phrases such as *destructive, soulless, ugly mess, appalling mess, most effective, we should demand,* and the repetition of the word *goal* in the last paragraph clearly indicate where his sympathies are (zoning regulations that would promote density in urban cores and mixed-use development) and are not (sprawl).

These sentences not only give you the main idea, but they also tell you nearly everything you need to know to quickly answer #12, #15, and #16 – none of which asks about the point directly.

In #12, knowing that the author is pro-regulation allows you to jump directly to (J). In #15, knowing that the author believes superstores move development away from downtown areas allows you to jump directly to (B), the only answer consistent with that idea. And in #16, you can make a very educated guess that (H) is correct based on process of elimination. If you know that the author is in favor of mixed-use developments, you can cross out (F). (G) can be eliminated because the author clearly indicates in the conclusion that *new* zoning laws are required. And in (J), "food" and "healthcare" are off-topic because the passage focuses on sprawl.

Primary Purpose

Unlike the main point, which tells you the essential idea or argument the author wants to convey, the primary purpose is the **rhetorical goal** or **function** of a passage or paragraph – it answers the question "Why did the author write this?" These questions may directly ask what the purpose of a paragraph/passage is, or they may ask what a particular section of the passage "serves to" accomplish. Some common purposes include explaining, analyzing, discussing, describing, and comparing.

In general, correct answers to primary purpose questions contain **neutral** purpose words such as *explain* or *illustrate* rather than *praise* or *promote*. Even though authors may have a positive or negative attitude toward a topic, they tend to remain relatively detached and objective. As a result, any answer that suggests a high level of emotional involvement is unlikely to be correct. Unless such an answer clearly corresponds to the content of the passage, you can generally assume that it will be wrong and start off by eliminating it. "Emotional" answers do not appear frequently – more often than not, all four answers will be phrased neutrally – but when they do, they can be useful tools for quick elimination. You can also play positive/negative: when a passage is clearly positive, you can immediately eliminate negative answers and vice versa.

Whenever the big picture is involved, you should also pay attention to **scope** – that is, whether the passage focuses on one specific thing/person (more likely) or things/people in general (less likely). For example, question #21 on p. 76 of *The Official Guide, 2018* plays on that concept. The passage itself focuses on the paintings of exactly one artist (Winslow Homer), but (B) refers to *fine arts* as a whole, and (D) refers to *artists*, plural.

In addition, you should **be careful with answers that refer to comparing and contrasting**. The vast majority of ACT passages focus on a single person, movement, theory, or work of art. While the author may on occasion include a comparison, the comparison will not actually be the goal of the passage. Rather, it will be mentioned to support a larger point. This type of answer choice requires you to distinguish between primary and secondary information – information that constitutes the main focus of the passage vs. information that is merely included in the passage.

Now let's look at how to work through some sample main-idea and primary-purpose questions.

European zoos of the late 19th and early 20th centuries incorporated the visual cultures of their animals' native homes into ornate buildings — reflections of their nations' colonial aspirations. The
5 Berlin Zoo's ostrich house resembled an Egyptian temple, with large columns flanking the entrance and scenes of ostrich hunts decorating the exterior. Berlin's elephant enclosure was built in the spirit of a Hindu temple; the home for its giraffes adopted an
10 Islamic architectural style. Zoos in Cologne, Lisbon, Antwerp, and Budapest, among others, created similar exhibits. These zoos were no home for subtlety: The animals they contained were exotic to most visitors; the buildings that did the containing
15 reinforced the sensation.

1. Which of the following best states the main idea of the paragraph?

   A. Buildings in late 19th and early 20th European zoos emphasized the exotic origins of the animals they housed.
   B. Many buildings in late 19th and early 20th century European zoos were built to resemble Egyptian temples.
   C. European zoos in the late 19th and early 20th centuries sought to evoke subtle emotions in their visitors.
   D. During the late 19th and early 20th centuries, most of the animals in European zoos came from outside of Europe.

Let's start by thinking about where the information necessary to answer the question is likely to be located. It's a main-idea question, and main ideas of paragraph are usually located at the beginning of the passage, in the topic sentence. That means we're going to start by focusing there:

> European zoos of the late 19th and early 20th centuries incorporated the visual cultures of their animals' native homes into ornate buildings — reflections of their nations' colonial aspirations.

The statement is pretty long and complex, so we're going to put it into our own words in order to simplify it. In its simplest form, it essentially states that European zoo buildings looked something like buildings in the animals' native countries. Even if you're not 100% sure what the sentence is saying, you can probably figure out that it's talking about buildings. But if you want some more information, you can also skip to the end of the paragraph and read the last sentence as well:

> These zoos were no home for subtlety: The animals they contained were exotic to most visitors; the buildings that did the containing reinforced the sensation.

Again, the focus is on buildings, so you can assume that the correct answer will be related to them. Only (A) and (B) mention buildings, so (C) and (D) can be eliminated immediately.

If that's too much of a stretch for you based on only two sentences, think about (C) and (D) this way: in (C), the word "subtle" does appear in the passage, but in a completely different context (*These zoos were no home for subtlety*). The answer is completely unrelated to the passage.

Be careful with (D): the passage does clearly imply that the animals came from outside Europe, but that's not its main focus. Not only do the first and last sentences mention buildings, but the body of the paragraph also refers to the *ostrich house*, the *elephant enclosure*, and an *Islamic architectural style* – all things related to buildings, not to animals. So (D) can be eliminated as well.

Next, think about what (A) and (B) are saying. (A) is consistent with both the first and the last sentences: the buildings "reinforced" the sensation that the animals were exotic. So that fits. On the other hand, (B) states that "many" European zoos had buildings that resembled Egyptian temples, whereas the passage only states that the *Berlin zoo's ostrich house* resembled an Egyptian temple. It's way too much of a leap to assume that the same was true for *many zoo buildings*. So (A) is correct.

Now let's look at the same passage from a slightly different angle:

European zoos of the late 19th and early 20th centuries incorporated the visual cultures of their animals' native homes into ornate buildings — reflections of their nations' colonial aspirations. The
5   Berlin Zoo's ostrich house resembled an Egyptian temple, with large columns flanking the entrance and scenes of ostrich hunts decorating the exterior. Berlin's elephant enclosure was built in the spirit of a Hindu temple; the home for its giraffes adopted an
10   Islamic architectural style. Zoos in Cologne, Lisbon, Antwerp, and Budapest, among others, created similar exhibits. These zoos were no home for subtlety: The animals they contained were exotic to most visitors; the buildings that did the containing
15   reinforced the sensation.

1.   The primary purpose of the paragraph is to:

   A.   argue that European zoos of the late 19th and early 20th centuries should have made more of an effort to accommodate their animals' needs.
   B.   describe specific ways in which late 19th and early 20th century European zoo buildings evoked the animals' home countries.
   C.   compare the buildings at the Berlin Zoo to zoo buildings in Cologne, Lisbon, Antwerp, and Budapest.
   D.   illustrate the importance of housing zoo animals in buildings that recreate their native homes.

The most effective way to approach this question is to think about how the paragraph is organized: the topic sentence presents an idea (buildings in late nineteenth- and early twentieth-century European zoos contained elements inspired by the "exotic" countries from which their animals came), and the rest of the paragraph is devoted to specific examples that support that idea (Berlin zoo ostrich house = Egyptian temple, elephant enclosure = Hindu temple, giraffes = Islamic architecture, etc.). That's exactly what (B) says, so it is correct. Notice that again, the key information is found in the topic sentence. The correct answer paraphrases the first sentence and presents it in context of the paragraph's function (*describe*).

If you'd rather play process of elimination, you can do so as well.

(A): The paragraph mentions nothing about zoos' efforts to accommodate animals' needs. In fact, it says nothing about animals' needs at all. The entire focus is on the zoo *buildings*, not the animals they housed.

In addition, the word "argue" is a tip-off that this answer is probably wrong. Most ACT Reading passages simply describe events, people, phenomena, etc. While some of the people discussed in a passage may argue in favor of a particular belief or position, that is usually not the case for the *author*. Unless it is exceedingly clear that the author strongly supports (or doesn't support) a given position, you can assume that any function or purpose question that begins with the word *argue* is likely to be incorrect.

(B): See above.

(C): Be careful with this answer. The paragraph does mention zoo buildings in all of those cities, but it doesn't compare them to one another. Rather, they're used as examples of buildings that *incorporated the visual cultures of their animals' native homes.*

(D): Again, this answer takes words from the paragraph and twists them to mean something different. The paragraph does mention the animals' *native homes,* but it says nothing about the importance of housing animals in buildings resembling those homes. In fact, that idea is entirely absent from the paragraph.

Starting on the next page, we're going to look at how paragraph main-idea questions work in the context of a complete passage.

A barn. A warehouse. A closet. These locations have something in common: They all contained films or parts of films that were missing and presumed lost forever. According to reliable estimates, at least 50 percent of all films made for public exhibition before 1950 have been lost. Move into the silent era, and the estimate shoots up to 90 percent. The cellulose nitrate film on which movies were recorded until 1950 is flammable and highly susceptible to deterioration. The medium that replaced nitrate, cellulose acetate, solved the flammability problem, but is vulnerable to disintegration, shrinkage, and breakage.

Film needs to be stored in a temperature and moisture controlled environment. Film archives all over the world maintain such climate-controlled storage facilities as a first line of defense. Transferring nitrate film to stable safety stock is a second precaution film preservationists take.

Actual restoration is a further, complicated step that many films will never undergo. Restoring celluloid films is a costly, time-consuming process that requires expert handling in one of the few photochemical labs that still exist; today, more films are being restored through digital correction, but this work is also labor-intensive.

The work also requires old-fashioned research. Film is an art form that everyone from producers to theater owners has felt entitled to alter to fit their requirements, including shortening films to maximize the number of screenings and cutting out material the exhibitor deemed inappropriate. Therefore, research must be done to find shooting scripts, directors' notes, and other preproduction materials to ensure the restoration is as complete as possible.

Established in 1990 by Martin Scorsese, the Film Foundation helps to conserve motion picture history by supporting preservation and restoration projects at film archives. The foundation has helped save more than 560 motion pictures. It prioritizes funding each year according to physical urgency. Also taken into account is the significance of a project, whether the film is an important work of a writer, actor, or director, or a technical first, or whether it approaches some social issue ahead of its time.

At its core, the Film Foundation represents a natural progression for Scorsese, arguably the world's greatest film enthusiast. Margaret Bodde, a film producer and executive director of the Film Foundation, says, "With Marty, what is so remarkable is his dedication to preservation and film as culture and an art form. He doesn't do it as an obligation; he does it because he wants future generations to be as inspired by film as he was."

Scorsese's storied career gained its inspiration from the numerous films he viewed growing up in Manhattan's Little Italy. One film that inspired Scorsese with a model for how to shoot the fight sequences in his 1980 film *Raging Bull* was *The Red Shoes* (1948), the ballet-centered masterpiece created by the powerhouse British directing team of Michael Powell and Emeric Pressburger. The Film Foundation funded its restoration in 2006, the first fully digital restoration with which it was involved.

Working from the original film negatives, preservationists found that tiny imperfections from the original film development had been exacerbated by time. In addition, much of the film had shrunk. Colors flickered, became mottled, and showed other types of distortion. The film also showed red, blue, and green specks throughout. Worst of all, mold had damaged the negatives.

After the film underwent an extensive cleaning process, it was digitized: 579,000 individual frames had to be scanned. Colors were reregistered, scratches smoothed, flecks removed, and color inconsistencies addressed. Last, a new filmstrip was produced.

The rapid shift from photochemical to digital production has raised concerns. Bodde says, "If a film is born digital, there should be a film output" because of the possibility of data corruption or the unavailability of playback mechanisms. The Film Foundation is working with archivists, technologists, and preservationists to ensure that photochemical preservation continues.

The foundation also offers an interdisciplinary curriculum to help develop visual literacy and film knowledge. This curriculum, The Story of Movies, has been embraced by well over thirty thousand schools. All of this effort works to ensure that future generations know the wonder of watching Moira Shearer move through the vivid, Technicolor dreamscapes of *The Red Shoes* and many other treasures of our film heritage.

Let's start by looking at an individual paragraph. As discussed earlier, questions that focus on specific paragraphs can ask about either the paragraphs themselves OR the role that they play within the passage as a whole. Since we've already discussed the former, we're now going to look at some examples of the latter.

1. The function of the fifth paragraph (lines 35-43) in relation to the passage as a whole is to:

OR:

The function of the fifth paragraph (lines 35-43) in relation to the fourth paragraph is to:

A. outline some of the processes that Martin Scorsese's Film Foundation uses to restore films.
B. discuss some of the social issues that are raised in films restored by Martin Scorsese's Film Foundation.
C. shift the focus of the passage from a broad discussion of film restoration to a specific organization that restores films.
D. describe how Martin Scorsese was inspired to establish the Film Foundation in 1990.

This is a true function question because the correct answer depends not only on the content of the paragraph, but also on the role that it plays in the passage as a whole. As discussed in Chapter 4, the fifth paragraph functions as a pivot point in the passage: it marks the beginning of the second major section, in which the focus of the passage moves from a general discussion of the difficulties of restoring films to a more specific focus on Martin Scorsese's Film Foundation (= a specific organization; don't get thrown off by the slightly more general wording). The answer is therefore (C). Note that if you marked that shift as you read through the passage, your work would be done.

If it is too confusing for you to think about structure as you do an initial read-through, however, you can still obtain the necessary information by rereading a shorter section of the passage when you go to answer the question. Since the question is asking about role of the paragraph *in context*, you need to establish some basic context by looking at the previous paragraph. Often, the last sentence or couple of sentences will give you enough to go on, but sometimes you will have to read more – the only thing that matters is that you obtain enough context for the reading to make sense. You then want to read the beginning of the paragraph in question, noticing how it changes from the end of the previous paragraph.

Let's just look at those two places right now:

> *Therefore, research must be done to find shooting scripts, directors' notes, and other preproduction materials to ensure the restoration is as complete as possible.*

> *Established in 1990 by Martin Scorsese, the Film Foundation helps to conserve motion picture history by supporting preservation and restoration projects at film archives.*

At first glance, the last sentence of the fourth paragraph might not seem to give you any information.

When you read the first sentence of the fifth paragraph, however, you can see that there's a shift. How do you know this? Because the sentence begins with the words *Established in 1990*.

Furthermore, the sentence provides an overview of what the Film Foundation is and what it does – information that clearly indicates that the author is introducing a new topic. The only answer that corresponds to that fact is (C): by definition, introducing a new topic means shifting focus. This type of shortcut requires you to read very actively, but if you are willing and able to do so, it can save you enormous amounts of time.

Alternately, you can of course play process of elimination. This can of course be a very effective strategy, but the danger with this type of question is that you might not recognize the correct answer when you see it and, as a result, eliminate it without really considering what it's saying. In my experience, students who are unaccustomed to thinking about texts in terms of organization and shifts in focus often jump to eliminate answers framed that way because they find them confusing or think they sound strange (or, less generously, because they don't really want to take the time to check them out).

You should not, however, ever eliminate an answer choice simply because you do not understand what it means, nor should you choose an answer only because you do understand what it means. Your ability to understand an answer has no – I repeat, *no* – effect whatsoever on whether that answer is correct or incorrect. When you find an answer confusing, you should leave it and focus on the answers you do understand. If you can eliminate them, then the confusing answer must be correct by default.

So that said, let's consider the choices one by one:

A. outline some of the processes that Martin Scorsese's Film
Foundation uses to restore films.

No. The paragraph introduces the Film Foundation and explains how it selects films, but it says absolutely nothing about how the Foundation actually goes about restoring those films.

B. discuss some of the social issues that are raised in films
restored by Martin Scorsese's Film Foundation.

Again, no. The paragraph only states that the Foundation takes into account *whether [a film] approaches some social issue ahead of its time.* It never actually discusses any of those issues.

C. shift the focus of the passage from a broad discussion of
film restoration to a specific organization that restores films.

See the analysis on the previous page. If you're confused, leave it.

D. describe how Martin Scorsese was inspired to establish
the Film Foundation in 1990.

No. The paragraph states that Scorsese established the Foundation in 1990, but it says nothing about what inspired him to do so.

That leaves (C). Even if you're confused by the wording of that answer, it's the only option.

Answers to function-in-context questions can also come from a slightly different angle:

2. The function of the fifth paragraph (lines 35-43) in
    relation to the passage as a whole is to:

    F. discuss some of the films that Martin Scorsese's Film
        Foundation has helped to save.
    G. outline the steps that film archives take to restore and
        preserve films.
    H. describe the factors that the Film Foundation takes into
        account when selecting films for restoration.
    J. explain how establishment of the Film Foundation has
        led to an increase in film viewership.

Although (H), the correct answer to this version of the question, is more straightforward, it is also somewhat deceptive. The question asks about the *function* of the fifth paragraph in relation to the whole passage, but the answer is actually based on the *content* of the fifth paragraph.

In addition, the information necessary to answer the question is not located in a usual key place (first sentence, last sentence) but is rather embedded in the body of the paragraph. (*It prioritizes funding each year according to physical urgency. Also taken into account is the significance of a project, whether the film is an important work of a writer, actor, or director, or a technical first, or whether it approaches some social issue ahead of its time.*) If you tried to answer this question by focusing on the start of the paragraph, you would be out of luck. Checking there initially would be a reasonable approach, but in this case, you would need to be flexible and ultimately look elsewhere.

You could also play process of elimination:

    F. discuss some of the films that Martin Scorsese's Film
        Foundation has helped to save.

No. The paragraph does not give specific examples of films restored by the Film Foundation.

    G. outline the steps that film archives take to restore and
        preserve films.

No. The paragraph states only that the film archives restore and preserve films; it never explains the process by which those things occur.

    H. describe the factors that the Film Foundation takes into
        account when selecting films for restoration.

Even though this idea is not introduced until the third sentence, the paragraph explicitly addresses the three factors (physical urgency, significance, social issues) that influence the Film Foundation's decision about which films to fund. Even if you're not sure, leave it.

    J. explain how establishment of the Film Foundation has
        led to an increase in film viewership.

No. The paragraph never even mentions film viewership, never mind how it was affected by the establishment of the Film Foundation. So (H) is the only possible answer.

Now let's consider a question that asks about the passage as a whole. These questions can be challenging because they ask you to distinguish between main ideas and details. It is not enough to recognize what an author said or why; rather, you must determine whether an idea is of primary or secondary importance. Incorrect answers may make factual statements about people, places, dates, etc. that are supported by the passage, but those answers will still be wrong because they do not identify the main focus of the passage.

It can therefore be helpful to think about ideas in terms of general vs. specific. If a passage focuses on a specific person, place, event, etc. and the answer choice is very general (e.g., the passage discusses a particular film and the answer refers to "films"), it's probably wrong. Likewise, if a passage is general and an answer choice is very specific, you can assume that it's incorrect.

When you read a passage as a series of details, questions that ask about the big picture can easily catch you off guard. If you're a strong reader, you'll probably get to the answer eventually through process of elimination, but you'll also waste time and leave yourself open to second-guessing.

So let's start with a **shortcut**: Before you look at the answer choices, go back and remind yourself what the passage is literally about. Even if you don't know exactly how the correct answer will be phrased, you can be pretty sure that it will be directly related to the topic of the passage.

In this case, you might say something like "restoring films" or "film preservation." If you want to take it a step further and add a bit more information, you might say something like "restoring films is hard." So the correct answer must be related to that general idea.

Keep that in mind when you look at the question below.

3. The primary purpose of the passage is to:

    A. compare the way that films were preserved prior to 1990 to the way that they are preserved today.
    B. discuss some of the problems involved in transferring film from photochemical to digital format.
    C. trace the steps involved in a film restoration, from initial cleaning to digitization.
    D. indicate some of the challenges involved in restoring film and describe how one organization has confronted those challenges.

The only answer choice directly consistent with the idea that restoring films is difficult is (D).

If you find it helpful, you can also think about how the passage is divided and what each section focuses on. The first section discusses some general problems involved in film restoration, and the second focuses on the important role that the Film Foundation has played in restoring films. That's basically what (D) says, so it's the answer.

For **an even shorter shortcut**, you can think about the fact that a very large portion of the passage is devoted to discussing the Film Foundation. Again, (D) is the only answer choice that refers to it, albeit in more general wording (*one organization*).

Otherwise, you can go through the answers one-by-one, being careful to consider whether each option merely includes information *mentioned* in the passage, or whether it accurately describes the passage as a whole.

A. compare the way that films were preserved prior to 1990
to the way that they are preserved today.

Be careful with this answer. The passage mentions that the Film Foundation was established in 1990, and it also mentions that the Film Foundation did its first digital restoration in 2006, but it says nothing to indicate that films *in general* are restored differently than they were before 1990. Besides, aside from briefly suggesting that films today can be preserved digitally, the passage does not offer a direct comparison between current and previous types of preservation.

B. discuss some of the problems involved in transferring
film from photochemical to digital format.

This answer is far too specific. The passage does discuss some of these issues in the second-to-last paragraph (lines 78-84), but the discussion is limited to one paragraph. If you want to check that out, you can scan the passage for the words *photochemical* or *digital*. If you don't see the words in question all over the place, the passage isn't about them.

C. trace the steps involved in a film restoration, from initial
cleaning to digitization.

Again, don't confuse "mentioning" and "being about." The passage does in fact discuss the restoration process in the second and third paragraphs, but again, the discussion is pretty much restricted to those paragraphs. And if it's restricted to one place, it can't be the primary purpose.

D. indicate some of the challenges involved in restoring
films and describe how one organization has confronted
those challenges.

Yes. As discussed, the two parts of the answer choice correspond to the two main parts of the passage: presentation of a problem (restoring films is hard), and discussion of what one particular organization (the Film Foundation) is doing to help resolve that problem. Again, the answer is (D).

On the next page, we're going to look at one more passage.

During the years I spent in the company of Alexander Graham Bell, at work on his biography, I often wondered what the inventor of the world's most important acoustical device—the telephone—might have sounded like.

Born in Scotland in 1847, Bell, at different periods of his life, lived in England, then Canada and, later, the Eastern Seaboard of the United States. His favorite refuge was Cape Breton Island, Nova Scotia, where he spent the summers from the mid-1880s on. In his day, 85 percent of the population there conversed in Gaelic. Did Bell speak with a Scottish burr? What was the pitch and depth of the voice with which he loved to belt out ballads and music hall songs?

Someone who knew that voice was his granddaughter, Mabel Grosvenor, a noted Washington, D.C. pediatrician who retired in 1966. In 2004, I met with Dr. Mabel, as she was known in the family, when she was 99 years old—clearheaded, dignified and a bit fierce. I inquired whether her grandfather had an accent. "He sounded," she said firmly, "like you." As a British-born immigrant to Canada, my accent is BBC English with a Canadian overlay: It made instant sense to me that I would share intonations and pronunciations with a man raised in Edinburgh who had resided in North America from the age of 23. When Dr. Mabel died in 2006, the last direct link with the inventor was gone.

Today, however, a dramatic application of digital technology has allowed researchers to recover Bell's voice from a recording held by the Smithsonian—a breakthrough announced here for the first time. From the 1880s on, until his death in 1922, Bell gave an extensive collection of laboratory materials to the Smithsonian Institution, where he was a member of the Board of Regents. The donation included more than 400 discs and cylinders Bell used as he tried his hand at recording sound. The holdings also documented Bell's research, should patent disputes arise similar to the protracted legal wrangling that attended the invention of the telephone.

Bell conducted his sound experiments between 1880 and 1886, collaborating with his cousin Chichester Bell and technician Charles Sumner Tainter. They worked at Bell's Volta Laboratory, at 1221 Connecticut Avenue in Washington, originally established inside what had been a stable. In 1877, his great rival, Thomas Edison, had recorded sound on embossed foil; Bell was eager to improve the process. Some of Bell's research on light and sound during this period anticipated fiber-optic communications.

Inside the lab, Bell and his associates bent over their pioneering audio apparatus, testing the potential of a variety of materials, including metal, wax, glass, paper, plaster, foil and cardboard, for recording sound, and then listening to what they had embedded on discs or cylinders. However, the precise methods they employed in early efforts to play back their recordings are lost to history.

As a result, says curator Carlene Stephens of the National Museum of American History, the discs, ranging from 4 to 14 inches in diameter, remained "mute artifacts." She began to wonder, she adds, "if we would ever know what was on them."

Then, Stephens learned that physicist Carl Haber at the Lawrence Berkeley National Laboratory in Berkeley, California, had succeeded in extracting sound from early recordings made in Paris in 1860. He and his team created high-resolution optical scans converted by computer into an audio file.

Stephens contacted Haber. Early in 2011, Haber, his colleague physicist Earl Cornell and Peter Alyea, a digital conversion specialist at the Library of Congress, began analyzing the Volta Lab discs, unlocking sound inaccessible for more than a century. Muffled voices could be detected reciting Hamlet's soliloquy, sequences of numbers and "Mary Had a Little Lamb."

In autumn 2011, Patrick Feaster, an Indiana University sound-media historian, aided by Stephens, compiled an exhaustive inventory of notations on the discs and cylinders—many scratched on wax and all but illegible. Their scholarly detective work led to a tantalizing discovery. Documents indicated that one wax-and-cardboard disc, from April 15, 1885—a date now deciphered from a wax inscription—contained a recording of Bell speaking.

On June 20, 2012, at the Library of Congress, a team including Haber, Stephens and Alyea was transfixed as it listened to the inventor himself: "In witness whereof—hear my voice, Alexander Graham Bell." In that ringing declaration, I heard the clear diction of a man whose father, Alexander Melville Bell, had been a renowned elocution teacher (and perhaps the model for the imperious Prof. Henry Higgins, in George Bernard Shaw's Pygmalion; Shaw acknowledged Bell in his preface to the play).

I heard, too, the deliberate enunciation of a devoted husband whose deaf wife, Mabel, was dependent on lip reading. And true to his granddaughter's word, the intonation of the British Isles was unmistakable in Bell's speech. The voice is vigorous and forthright—as was the inventor, at last speaking to us across the years.

STOP!

Who or what is the topic of this passage? If you're not sure, remember to look for the word that appears throughout the passage.

_____

_____

Summarize the passage in 3-5 words. (You don't need to write a full sentence.)

_____

_____

1. The primary purpose of the passage is to:

   A. explain how the rivalry between Bell and Edison led to a series of important discoveries.
   B. praise Earl Cornell and Peter Alyea for their success in revealing Bell's voice.
   C. discuss how a new technology allowed Bell's voice to be revealed to modern listeners.
   D. describe how the author's conversation with Mabel Grosvenor led to the discovery of the disk with Bell's voice.

2. The main theme of the passage is that:

   F. familiar way of looking at a problem can sometimes yield unexpected results.
   G. developments in technology can be used to shed new light on the past.
   H. scientists are often as mysterious to their own families as they are to the public.
   J. people raised in different circumstances can nevertheless view the world in similar ways.

3. The function of the second paragraph (lines 6-14) in relation to the passage as a whole is to:

   What is this paragraph about?

   _____

   _____

   A. provide biographical information that suggests possible influences on Bell's speech.
   B. discuss how Bell's frequent moves influenced his personality.
   C. describe how Bell's accent evolved from childhood to adulthood.
   D. contrast a commonly held view of Bell with the view held by the author.

4. The function of the eleventh paragraph (lines 93-101) in relation to the passage as a whole is to:

   What is this paragraph about?

   _____

   _____

   F. explore the relationship between technology and theater.
   G. point out a major source of influence on George Bernard Shaw's works.
   H. indicate the result of a discovery mentioned in the previous paragraph.
   J. describe the author's reaction to hearing Bell's voice for the first time.

Answers are at the bottom of p. 75.

Supporting Evidence

Both main-idea and function questions test your ability to distinguish between primary and supporting information, but occasionally the ACT will test your understanding of those elements the other way around. Some questions, for example, will ask you to start with the supporting evidence and use it to identify the point that it illustrates. These are often paragraph main-idea questions.

Unfortunately, the evidence will not always be located next to the point it supports. It may be located several sentences later or in a different section of the passage entirely. Although you may find these questions irritating, they test a crucial aspect of comprehension: the ability to "track" an idea through a passage and to recognize that authors do not always present evidence sequentially. On the contrary, they may make a point, then briefly turn their attention to another (related) topic in order to provide clarification or introduce another consideration before returning to present evidence for the original claim.

For example, a main-point question could also be asked this way:

European zoos of the late 19th and early 20th centuries incorporated the visual cultures of their animals' native homes into ornate buildings — reflections of their nations' colonial aspirations. The
5 Berlin Zoo's ostrich house resembled an Egyptian temple, with large columns flanking the entrance and scenes of ostrich hunts decorating the exterior. Berlin's elephant enclosure was built in the spirit of a Hindu temple; the home for its giraffes adopted an
10 Islamic architectural style. Zoos in Cologne, Antwerp, and Budapest, among others, created similar exhibits. These zoos were no home for subtlety: The animals they contained were exotic to most visitors; the buildings that did the containing
15 reinforced the sensation.

1. The author mentions "Zoos in Cologne, Lisbon, Antwerp, and Budapest" (lines 10-11) in order to illustrate the point that:

   A. Buildings in late 19th and early 20th European zoos emphasized the exotic origins of the animals they housed.
   B. Many buildings in late 19th and early 20th century European zoos were built to resemble Egyptian temples.
   C. European zoos in the late 19th and early 20th centuries sought to evoke subtle emotions in their visitors.
   D. During the late 19th and early 20th centuries, most of the animals in European zoos came from outside of Europe.

Although the question cites lines 10-11, those lines are only important insofar as they support a larger point. They're located toward the end of the paragraph, so focus on the last sentence – the one most likely to reemphasize the point. That sentence tells us that the buildings *reinforced the sensation [that the buildings housing the animals were exotic]*, which corresponds to (A).

Other questions ask you which statement best supports (or is most similar to) an idea discussed elsewhere in the passage. The good news is that the ACT gives you some help: each answer choice typically indicates specific lines in the passage so that you do not have to spend time hunting on your own. That said, doing some basic legwork toward identifying the answer upfront can save you quite a lot of time and worry. That, however, requires you to approach the question actively, summarizing the point in your own words and thinking about what sort of information would most logically support it rather than relying on the answer choices to point you in the right direction.

(Re)read the passage on the following page. Then, look at the sample question on p. 75.

"A finite universe"—that's the phrase that Jim Kuhn uses to describe the surviving early quartos of Shakespeare's plays. It evokes something that seems more expansive and dynamic than the estimated 777 paperback-sized volumes that, for the last four hundred years, have physically carried our most direct evidence of the Bard's work. It also begins to suggest the appeal of those volumes in aggregate: There is an end to their universe, the texts that define it can be collected, and that collection, completed.

Five years ago, Kuhn, then head of collection information services at the Folger Shakespeare Library, helped to prototype just such a collection: a digital repository capable of bringing together in one location the sparse and geographically scattered universe of these rare Shakespeare texts. The project, which was led by the Folger and the University of Oxford, involved librarians, curators, computer scientists, educators, and interns from scholarly institutions on both sides of the Atlantic.

As a proof of concept, they tackled the thirty-two early copies of *Hamlet* held by the participating libraries (the Folger, the British Library, the Bodleian Library at Oxford, the Huntington Library, the National Library of Scotland, and the University of Edinburgh Library). Sixteen months spent gathering cover-to-cover digital images, producing transcriptions, and developing an online interface resulted, in November of 2009, in the Shakespeare Quartos Archive, which boasts the most comprehensive collection of early *Hamlets* available and is setting an example for newer literary archives such as the recently announced Shelley–Godwin Archive.

Among Shakespeare's works, *Hamlet* is an obvious choice for such an endeavor, not only because of the play's iconic status in literary and popular culture, but because many perplexities surround its textual transmission. "*Hamlet* goes from the stage to the printed page at one point or another," says Steven Galbraith, another former member of the SQA's Folger team; "but the printed page is, materially, what survives for us." We don't have an authorial manuscript (of *Hamlet* or any of the Bard's works) against which to judge those pages, and, as it turns out, we don't have an unassailably stable *Hamlet* in any form: We have *Hamlets*, plural—a circumstance that becomes amply clear when one turns to the surviving quartos themselves. Look closely enough, and not just every edition, but every copy differs from every other.

Helping readers get a good look at these quartos is where the SQA excels. Partnering with yet another scholarly institution (the Maryland Institute for Technology in the Humanities, which is part of the University of Maryland, College Park), the SQA team developed a web-based interface and set of digital tools designed for close, almost microscopic, comparative analysis. Among a number of other features, one can execute word searches on the texts, superimpose and adjust the transparency of page images, and run a difference algorithm that immediately highlights every inconsistency—including printers' marks, marginal notations, and other paratextual matter—between any two of the archive's scrupulously executed transcriptions. Armed with these tools, the "originals" can begin to look like a dense patchwork of inconsistency—*Hamlet*, hopelessly at odds with itself.

Galbraith, a curator by trade, has another perspective on the body of evidence that the SQA offers up, one that looks beyond the *Hamlet* texts themselves, to their value as archaeological specimens. "Every book has its own story," he says, "and using the SQA with a critical eye, you can really begin to see that. There are differences in bindings; different people have owned them and marked them up, used them in different ways." And the bigger question, he adds, the one to which all these differences lead, is one of provenance: "Where has this book been for the last four hundred years?" Tracing the hand or characteristic markings of some previous reader through the text, focusing on the passages or words that he or she focused on, identifying the binder or the most worn pages, one can begin to piece together the trajectories of these individual books through history and how they were used.

The SQA's collection of high-resolution and transcribed *Hamlets* may, with some clever detective work, prove a boon to literary scholars and bibliographers. But, as both Kuhn and Galbraith point out, the archive also helps to raise and answer questions touching on digitization efforts beyond Shakespeare: What do you do when the imaging and transcription are done? What can you do with the texts now that you couldn't do before? Neither the content of the plays—the lines, words, punctuation marks, paratextual matter, marginalia—nor the images of their physical medium necessarily suggest all of the uses to which the data might be put. Making the texts accessible, and, what is more important, accessible as data, opens them up to modes of analysis and creativity beyond those traditionally associated with the humanities. "The goal," says Galbraith, "is to release that data and let the scholars, directors, and artists, or whoever is coming to the quartos, do their work with them in whatever way, for whatever reason." One wonders what a statistician, digital artist, or data visualization expert might find in the SQA.

1. The author's statement that "many perplexities surround its textual transmission" (line 37) is best supported and illustrated by which of the following?

Sorry, but unfortunately you don't get to look at the answer choices quite yet. Before we get to that step, we're going to figure out just what the quotation in the question actually means. Notice that although the quote short, it's dense. And even though you might understand each word individually, you might not get what all of the words put together really mean.

So let's start off by trying to put together what the sentence is saying: *perplexing* means "puzzling," so *perplexities* are things that are puzzling. *Textual* means having to do with texts, and the passage is talking about *Hamlet*, so logically this refers to the text of *Hamlet*. Finally, *transmission* refers to how things – in this case, a play – are passed from person to person. So the phrase is basically saying that there are a lot of things people don't understand about how the text of *Hamlet* was transmitted. The following sentences clarify that statement by explaining that no single, definitive version of *Hamlet* was ever printed, just lots of different versions from different productions. **The correct answer must therefore be consistent with the idea that there are lots of different versions of the play.** One by one, we're going to check out the options and see whether they meet that criterion.

    A. Sixteen months spent gathering cover-to-cover digital images, producing transcriptions, and developing an online interface (lines 25-27).

No. This is about how long it took to produce the Shakespeare Quarto Archive. It is completely unrelated to the fact that there are multiple versions of the play.

    B. not just every edition, but every copy differs from every other (lines 47-48).

Yes, this makes sense. If you go back and read the full sentence, you'll see that it refers to *Hamlet*. The fact that every copy is different is perfectly consistent with the idea that there is no definitive version of the play. If you want to look at the other answers just to be 100% sure, you can – but since you've already figured out what the correct answer must say and determined that this one fits, you're probably better off picking it and moving on.

    C. Among a number of other features, one can execute word searches on the texts (lines 56-57).

No. This is about the kinds of research that one can do in the Shakespeare Quarto Archive. It's completely off-topic.

    D. one can begin to piece together the trajectories of these individual books through history and how they were used (lines 80-82).

No. Don't get distracted by the reference to *individual books*. The focus is on how copies of the play have changed hands throughout history, not about the lack of a definitive version.

So the answer is (B).

(Answers from exercises on p. 72: 1C, 2G, 3A, 4H)

7   Vocabulary in Context

Vocabulary-in-context questions are usually among the more straightforward questions, as well as some of the least time-consuming. Unlike most other question types, they are essentially guaranteed to indicate the line in which a given word appears; you do not have to spend time searching for the necessary information. If timing is a consistent problem for you, vocabulary-in-context questions should be among the first questions you answer.

The most important thing to understand about vocabulary-in-context questions is that they are just that – they do not test dictionary definitions, but rather how words and phrases are used in the context of actual pieces of writing. As a result, **you do not need to know the exact definitions of the words tested – you only need to understand how those words are used in the particular places in question and be able to recognize synonyms for them** (or be able to determine synonyms for them by process of elimination).

You can therefore think of a question that asks, "As it is used in line 45, the word *confused* most nearly means…" as saying, "As it is used in line 45, the word ------- most nearly means…" If it helps, you can even take your pencil and cross out the word in the passage.

Keep in mind that the majority of the words tested will not be used in their most common definition – there would be little point in testing them that way. Consequently, **if you see the literal definition provided as an answer choice, you can assume that it is incorrect.**

If you do not spot the answer immediately, there are a few different strategies you can use:

1) **Read the appropriate section of the passage carefully and plug in your own word, then check the answer choices and find the one that most closely matches.**

    The major potential weaknesses of this strategy are that 1) you will not plug in a word that truly fits, or 2) you will plug in an acceptable word but not recognize the similarity between it and the correct answer choice. If you are a strong reader with a solid vocabulary, however, this is usually an effective strategy.

2) **Plug each answer choice into the passage and read it in context.**

    You will often be able to hear that one answer sounds correct and makes sense in context or, at the very least, that one or more of the incorrect answers clearly do not make sense.

3) **Play positive/negative.**

    If the surrounding information in the passage is clearly positive, you can eliminate any negative answer and vice versa.

Example #1

For all of modern history, a small, carnivorous
South American mammal in the raccoon family has
evaded the scientific community. Untold thousands of
these red, furry creatures scampered through the trees
5 of the Andean cloud forests, but they did so at night,
hidden by dense fog. Nearly two dozen preserved
samples—mostly skulls or furs—were mislabeled in
museum collections across the United States. There's
even evidence that one individual lived in several
10 American zoos during the 1960s—its keepers were
mystified as to why it refused to breed with its peers.

1. As it is used in line 3, the word *evaded* most
    nearly means:

    A. devalued.
    B. eluded.
    C. confirmed.
    D. exploited.

Remember: it doesn't matter whether you know what *evaded* means – the passage is set up so that you can figure it out. The real question is whether you can determine which one of the answers makes the most sense in context.

Let's consider what we know. The sentence in which the word appears doesn't give us a whole lot of information, but if we look at the next sentence, we get some important clues. The animal in question *scampered through the trees…at night, hidden by dense fog.* If something is "hidden by fog," it can't be seen.

Given that knowledge, it's reasonable to assume that *evaded* means something slightly negative like "hid from" or "avoided." If you know that's the definition of *eluded*, then you can pick (B) and be done. If not, play process of elimination. *Confirmed* is positive and means the opposite of the word you're looking for, eliminating (C). *Devalued* and *exploited* (took advantage of) don't fit with the idea of being hidden by dense fog, so they can be eliminated as well. So even if you're not entirely sure about *eluded*, you can still pick (B).

Example #2:

Douglas Keister has spent the past four
decades traveling the country to photograph
subjects as varied as architecture, folk art and
cemeteries. Over the years, as he moved from his
5 hometown of Lincoln, Nebraska, to several
different cities in California, he carted around a
heavy box of 280 antique glass-plate negatives that
he'd bought when he was 17 from a friend who'd
found them at a garage sale. "I thought, 'Why the
10 heck am I keeping these things?'" he says.

2. As it is used in line 6, the word *carted*
    most nearly means:

    A. constructed.
    B. removed.
    C. hauled.
    D. demonstrated.

In this case, the sentence in which the word *cart* appears gives us some clues. If Keister *moved* from Nebraska to California, then the word in question must also mean something like "moved." And the fact that the box was *heavy* and contained *280 glass-plate negatives* tells us that it was probably big and not very easy to transport. So we're looking for a word consistent with that idea.

Constructed, removed, and *demonstrated* are all unrelated to moving a heavy object, whereas *hauled* is typically used to convey just that idea. That makes the answer (C).

Recognizing Definitions

Most vocabulary-in-context questions ask you to identify a synonym for a word in the passage, but some questions will test vocabulary the other way around – that is, the passage will provide a definition or description, and you must identify the word being defined or described from among the answer choices.

For example, let's look at this passage from a slightly different angle:

> For all of modern history, a small, carnivorous South American mammal in the raccoon family has evaded the scientific community. Untold thousands of these red, furry creatures scampered through the trees
> 5 of the Andean cloud forests, but they did so at night, hidden by dense fog. Nearly two-dozen preserved samples—mostly skulls or furs—were mislabeled in museum collections across the United States. There's even evidence that one individual lived in several
> 10 American zoos during the 1960s—its keepers were mystified as to why it refused to breed with its peers.

1. Lines 1-11 suggest that the scientific community regarded the South American mammal as:

    A. enigmatic.
    B. threatening.
    C. adaptable.
    D. endangered.

Now, instead of focusing on context clues for a single word, you must find the information that describes what scientists think about the mammal. The first and last sentences of a paragraph are usually important, you want to pay close attention to them. What do they indicate? That the mammal *evaded the scientific community*, and *its keepers were mystified*. The correct answer must therefore mean something like "mysterious." That is the definition of *enigmatic*, so (A) is correct.

Even if you don't know what *enigmatic* means, you can still use the context clues and get to (A) by process of elimination. *Threatening, adaptable,* and *endangered* are words commonly associated with wild animals, but they are all entirely unrelated to mysteriousness. So once again, you're left with (A) as the only possible answer.

Alternately, you may need to know the definition of a word in the passage in order to answer the question, even if the question does not appear to directly test vocabulary.

> For all of modern history, a small, carnivorous South American mammal in the raccoon family has evaded the scientific community. Untold thousands of these red, furry creatures scampered through the trees
> 5 of the Andean cloud forests, but they did so at night, hidden by dense fog. Nearly two-dozen preserved samples—mostly skulls or furs—were mislabeled in museum collections across the United States. There's even evidence that one individual lived in several
> 10 American zoos during the 1960s—its keepers were mystified as to why it refused to breed with its peers.

1. The passage indicates that the scientific community:

    A. has only succeeded in studying the small, carnivorous South American mammal at night.
    B. has historically been prone to mislabeling specimens.
    C. is often unable to obtain important specimens from museums.
    D. has never examined the small, carnivorous South American mammal directly.

The key to the question is the word *evaded* – it means "avoided," indicating that scientists have been unable to examine the mammal. (D) is thus correct.

Now let's look at all those different question types in the context of a full passage.

During the years I spent in the company of Alexander Graham Bell, at work on his biography, I often wondered what the inventor of the world's most important acoustical device—the telephone—might have sounded like.

Born in Scotland in 1847, Bell, at different periods of his life, lived in England, then Canada and, later, the Eastern Seaboard of the United States. His favorite refuge was Cape Breton Island, Nova Scotia, where he spent the summers from the mid-1880s on. In his day, 85 percent of the population there conversed in Gaelic. Did Bell speak with a Scottish burr? What was the pitch and depth of the voice with which he loved to belt out ballads and music hall songs?

Someone who knew that voice was his granddaughter, Mabel Grosvenor, a noted Washington, D.C. pediatrician who retired in 1966. In 2004, I met with Dr. Mabel, as she was known in the family, when she was 99 years old—clearheaded, dignified and a bit fierce. I inquired whether her grandfather had an accent. "He sounded," she said firmly, "like you." As a British-born immigrant to Canada, my accent is BBC English with a Canadian overlay: It made instant sense to me that I would share intonations and pronunciations with a man raised in Edinburgh who had resided in North America from the age of 23. When Dr. Mabel died in 2006, the last direct link with the inventor was gone.

Today, however, a dramatic application of digital technology has allowed researchers to recover Bell's voice from a recording held by the Smithsonian—a breakthrough announced here for the first time. From the 1880s on, until his death in 1922, Bell gave an extensive collection of laboratory materials to the Smithsonian Institution, where he was a member of the Board of Regents. The donation included more than 400 discs and cylinders Bell used as he tried his hand at recording sound. The holdings also documented Bell's research, should patent disputes arise similar to the protracted legal wrangling that attended the invention of the telephone.

Bell conducted his sound experiments between 1880 and 1886, collaborating with his cousin Chichester Bell and technician Charles Sumner Tainter. They worked at Bell's Volta Laboratory, at 1221 Connecticut Avenue in Washington, originally established inside what had been a stable. In 1877, his great rival, Thomas Edison, had recorded sound on embossed foil; Bell was eager to improve the process. Some of Bell's research on light and sound during this period anticipated fiber-optic communications.

Inside the lab, Bell and his associates bent over their pioneering audio apparatus, testing the potential of a variety of materials, including metal, wax, glass, paper, plaster, foil and cardboard, for recording sound, and then listening to what they had embedded on discs or cylinders. However, the precise methods they employed in early efforts to play back their recordings are lost to history.

As a result, says curator Carlene Stephens of the National Museum of American History, the discs, ranging from 4 to 14 inches in diameter, remained "mute artifacts." She began to wonder, she adds, "if we would ever know what was on them."

Then, Stephens learned that physicist Carl Haber at the Lawrence Berkeley National Laboratory in Berkeley, California, had succeeded in extracting sound from early recordings made in Paris in 1860. He and his team created high-resolution optical scans converted by computer into an audio file.

Stephens contacted Haber. Early in 2011, Haber, his colleague physicist Earl Cornell and Peter Alyea, a digital conversion specialist at the Library of Congress, began analyzing the Volta Lab discs, unlocking sound inaccessible for more than a century. Muffled voices could be detected reciting Hamlet's soliloquy, sequences of numbers and "Mary Had a Little Lamb."

In autumn 2011, Patrick Feaster, an Indiana University sound-media historian, aided by Stephens, compiled an exhaustive inventory of notations on the discs and cylinders—many scratched on wax and all but illegible. Their scholarly detective work led to a tantalizing discovery. Documents indicated that one wax-and-cardboard disc, from April 15, 1885—a date now deciphered from a wax inscription—contained a recording of Bell speaking.

On June 20, 2012, at the Library of Congress, a team including Haber, Stephens and Alyea was transfixed as it listened to the inventor himself: "In witness whereof—hear my voice, Alexander Graham Bell." In that ringing declaration, I heard the clear diction of a man whose father, Alexander Melville Bell, had been a renowned elocution teacher (and perhaps the model for the imperious Prof. Henry Higgins, in George Bernard Shaw's Pygmalion; Shaw acknowledged Bell in his preface to the play).

I heard, too, the deliberate enunciation of a devoted husband whose deaf wife, Mabel, was dependent on lip reading. And true to his granddaughter's word, the intonation of the British Isles was unmistakable in Bell's speech. The voice is vigorous and forthright—as was the inventor, at last speaking to us across the years.

1. As it is used in line 22, the word *firmly* most nearly means:

   A. rigidly.
   B. loudly.
   C. decisively.
   D. tightly.

2. As it is used in line 40, the word *attended* most nearly means:

   F. appeared.
   G. accompanied.
   H. presented.
   J. visited.

3. As it is used in line 51, the word *anticipated* most nearly means:

   A. waited for.
   B. assumed.
   C. foreshadowed.
   D. resisted.

4. As it is used in line 99, the word *model* most nearly means:

   F. convention.
   G. standard.
   H. classic.
   J. example.

5. The passage indicates that Alexander Graham Bell's father:

   A. was famous for teaching elocution.
   B. was dependent on lip reading.
   C. had a unique cadence to his speech.
   D. was undoubtedly the inspiration for Henry Higgins.

6. According to the passage, Bell's invention of the telephone:

   F. involved lengthy legal disputes.
   G. came as a surprise to members of the Smithsonian Institution.
   H. resulted from his collaboration with Chichester Bell and Charles Sumner Tainter.
   J. took place at 1221 Connecticut Avenue in Washington.

7. As it is described in the passage, Alexander Graham Bell's voice can be best characterized as:

   A. anxious and tentative.
   B. strong and direct.
   C. clear and demanding.
   D. cloudy and muffled.

8   Reasonable Inferences

Inference questions tend to be among the more challenging types of Reading questions. Instead of testing your understanding of what *is* in the text, inference questions test your understanding of what *isn't* in the text. Rather than ask you what the passage states, inference questions ask you to identify what it **suggests** or **implies**, or what can be **reasonably inferred** from it. Correct answers to these questions are, however, directly implied by what the author does explicitly state. If you think logically and carefully, there is no reason for this type of question to be prohibitively difficult.

When working through inference questions, you must always make sure to keep in mind that **answers will not be located word-for-word in the passage but will instead require an extra step of reasoning**. As a result, you should not go back to the passage with the expectation of finding the answer stated literally; if you do so, you will end up not only wasting large amounts of time but also be reduced to guessing. Rather, you must be prepared to search for information relevant to the question at hand while keeping in mind that you are responsible for making the leap from the specific wording in the passage to the answer choice itself. Note that this is a very different process than that required by many ACT Reading questions, the answers to which are stated either word-for-word or very nearly word-for-word in the passage. If you are either pressed for time or mentally unready to shift your approach, you are better off skipping these questions and returning to them after you have answered the more straightforward questions.

Some inference questions will provide line numbers, but unfortunately that will not always be the case. Inference questions that do not provide line numbers thus test two skills simultaneously: your ability to think logically about where relevant information is most likely to be located, and your ability to draw reasonable conclusions based on the specific wording in the text.

What Makes an Inference "Reasonable?"

The most important thing to understand about inferences on the ACT is that they follow much stricter rules than the kinds of inferences you may be accustomed to making in English class. For example, if you read a novel in which a character is easily angered, you might assume that the author is suggesting that the character is a bad person, or that the author is warning the reader not to behave in the same way – whether or not there is direct support for those ideas in the text. This type of thinking will get you into a lot of trouble on the ACT. In reality, answers to inference questions often do nothing more than restate the same information that is in the text – they merely do so from a different angle and with different wording.

It is true that some inference questions will require you to make *slightly* bigger leaps. In every case, however, the passage will contain specific words or phrases that directly imply a particular idea or relationship. If you cannot point to a specific section of the passage that clearly supports a particular answer, that answer is probably not correct. Vague feelings about what an author *might* be trying to imply don't count.

For example, consider the following statement:

> *During the years I spent in the company of Alexander Graham Bell, at work on his biography, I often wondered what the inventor of the world's most important acoustical device—the telephone—might have sounded like.*

We can make several inferences from this sentence:

First, the fact that the author *wondered* what Alexander Graham Bell's voice sounded like directly implies that she never actually listened to Bell's voice. (If she had heard Bell's voice, she would know what it sounded like and would have no reason to wonder about it.) **The inference that the author never heard Bell's voice is reasonable because it is essentially contained in the words that the author does use.** It is only an inference because the author does not directly state that she never heard Bell speak.

We can also reasonably infer that Bell invented the telephone. Even though the author does not state that fact word-for-word, she directly implies it by indicating that she was at work on Bell's biography and then, in the next part of the sentence, by referring to *the inventor of the world's most important acoustical device.* The author could theoretically be referring to two different people; it is the reader's job to make the logical connection and recognize that both references denote the same individual. (The author wrote a biography of Bell, and people who have biographies written about them are usually very important. We can thus associate the phrase *world's most important acoustical device* with Bell.)

Furthermore, the phrase *world's most important acoustical device* directly implies that there are other acoustical devices less important than the telephone. You should always pay attention when inference questions involve the ideas of **more** and **less**. If the passage refers to "more," the correct answer is likely to refer to "less" (as is the case here) and vice versa.

Finally, we can reasonably infer that the author has a **positive attitude** toward Bell because she refers to him as the *inventor of the world's most important acoustical device* and because she indicates that she wrote a biography of him. The extremely positive language, coupled with the fact that the author spent her time writing a book about Bell, suggests that she holds him in very high regard.

We cannot, however, step outside the bounds of the text and make larger assumptions that the passage does not explicitly support. For example, the author states only that the telephone is the *most important acoustical* device. She does not, however, mention any other type of device. So we cannot, for instance, infer that she considers the telephone *the most important invention ever* – her assertion is **specific** to one field (acoustical devices), so that type of assumption is **far too general** (all inventions). Likewise, we cannot assume that the author considers Bell the most important inventor ever. All we know is that she believes Bell invented the most important type of *acoustical* device. We cannot by extension assume that she believes Bell invented the most important type of *communication* device, or that Bell was more important than inventors in other fields.

In fact, we can only make a generalization when the author does so in the text – in that case, the correct answer will essentially rephrase the passage itself. For an *Official Guide, 2018* example, look at question #29 on p. 373. The conclusion of Passage A clearly indicates that the narrator is focused on conveying the truth of a situation rather than the literal truth. Likewise, in passage B, the conclusion indicates that Hemingway distorted or interpreted facts in order to make them consistent with his version of the truth. Both statements essentially rephrase (C) – sometimes an artistic truth is more important than a strict adherence to reality. Same idea, different words.

"Date" and "Number" Questions

Questions that ask about various dates/time periods and numbers mentioned in a passage often have the potential to be both tricky and time-consuming if you're not prepared for how to tackle them. Tricky because they seem deceptively straightforward (test-takers typically assume that they must do nothing more than spot the correct date in the passage), and time-consuming because they are rarely as straightforward as they seem. In addition, they often require some additional (very simple) calculations.

Because dates and numbers make such good targets for inference questions, you should **circle any date or number** that you encounter while reading. If there are a lot of numbers/dates, however, you should probably not bother to circle every single one; you should use your judgment as to how many you can reasonably mark without losing focus.

To be fair, answers to some date- or number-based questions will appear directly in the passage, and you should not immediately panic when you see one. Many answers, however, will not be quite so obvious, and you should think twice about attempting them if you are running short for time.

Let's look at an example:

> One of the little-known turning points in the history of American travel occurred in the spring of *1869*, when a handsome young preacher from Boston named William H. H. Murray published one of the first guidebooks to a wilderness area. In describing the Adirondack Mountains—a 9,000-square-mile expanse of lakes, forests and rivers in upstate New York—Murray broached the then-outrageous idea that an excursion into raw nature could actually be pleasurable. **Before that date**, most Americans considered the country's primeval landscapes only as obstacles to be conquered. But Murray's self-help opus, Adventures in the Wilderness; or, Camp-Life in the Adirondacks, *suggested that hiking, canoeing and fishing in unsullied nature were the ultimate health tonic for harried city dwellers whose constitutions were weakened by the demands of civilized life.*

From an inference perspective, there are a couple of things to notice in this paragraph. First, there is the date *1869*, mentioned right at the beginning of the passage. Since it is the only date mentioned, there's a good chance that it will be important.

Second, in the fifth line, we encounter the phrase *Before that date*. Not only does it call attention to the date mentioned, but the phrasing itself makes it ideal for an inference question: events that are discussed in terms of **before** in a passage can easily be rephrased in terms of **after** for a correct answer – sometimes in ways that are obvious, and sometimes in ways that are not.

For example, you could see a question that looks like this:

It can reasonably inferred from the passage that people
would have regarded hiking, canoeing and fishing as
activities beneficial to their health in:

A. 1852.
B. 1857.
C. 1868.
D. 1875.

When most people encounter a question like this, their first instinct is to go back to the passage and try to find the answer stated word-for-word. Seeing the date *1869* and noticing that it's the only date that appears, they immediately assume it must be the correct answer. When they look at the answers, however, they discover that *1869* does not appear and immediately become confused. And because they aren't sure how to work through the question for real, they often end up guessing.

To understand what this question is really asking, we're going to take it apart and work through it step by step.

Because the question is worded in a fairly confusing manner, the first thing we want to do is to rephrase it in a simpler way. We could say something like "When did people think hiking, canoeing, and fishing were good for them?" That's much easier to manage than the original version.

Next, we want to go back to the passage and start working from the information we do have. The key phrase in the question is *hiking, canoeing, and fishing*, so we want to look for those words and then read the **entire sentence** in which they appear, as well as any surrounding information that's clearly relevant to the question.

The sentence itself doesn't really give us any information necessary to answer the question. The fact that it begins with the word *but* does, however, tell us that it's contradicting the information before it. So now we need to back up and read from the previous sentence.

> **Before that date**, *most Americans considered the country's primeval landscapes only as obstacles to be conquered. But Murray's self-help opus,* Adventures in the Wilderness; or, Camp-Life in the Adirondacks, *suggested that hiking, canoeing and fishing in unsullied nature were the ultimate health tonic for harried city dwellers whose constitutions were weakened by the demands of civilized life.*

Now we have something to work with. The previous sentence refers to *that date*, and since the only date mentioned in the passage is 1869, we know that it must be referring to 1869. So the first sentence is describing something that occurred **before** 1869, when Murray's book was published.

The word *but* at the start of the next sentence is very important because it tells us that the passage is shifting directions: it's describing the change in people's attitudes toward outdoor activities that occurred after Murray's book appeared – before the book appeared, people thought of the outdoors as an *[obstacle] to be conquered*, but afterwards, they thought of it as a *health tonic*.

Because the book appeared in 1869, that shift must have taken place **in** or **after** 1869. The correct answer must therefore refer to a date after 1869.

(A), (B), and (C) all refer to dates **before** 1869. Only 1875 came **after** 1869, making (D) the only possible answer.

Now let's look at some inference questions in the context of a full-length passage. Notice that there are a number of references to dates and other numbers. If you want to try circling those references as you read, you can do so. If, however, you find that looking out for them while trying to absorb the meaning of the passage is too confusing, you should not worry about trying to mark each one.

A barn. A warehouse. A closet. These locations have something in common: They all contained films or parts of films that were missing and presumed lost forever. According to reliable estimates, at least 50 percent of all films made for public exhibition before 1950 have been lost. Move into the silent era, and the estimate shoots up to 90 percent. The cellulose nitrate film on which movies were recorded until 1950 is flammable and highly susceptible to deterioration. The medium that replaced nitrate, cellulose acetate, solved the flammability problem, but is vulnerable to disintegration, shrinkage, and breakage.

Film needs to be stored in a temperature and moisture controlled environment. Film archives all over the world maintain such climate-controlled storage facilities as a first line of defense. Transferring nitrate film to stable safety stock is a second precaution film preservationists take.

Actual restoration is a further, complicated step that many films will never undergo. Restoring celluloid films is a costly, time-consuming process that requires expert handling in one of the few photochemical labs that still exist; today, more films are being restored through digital correction, but this work is also labor-intensive.

The work also requires old-fashioned research. Film is an art form that everyone from producers to theater owners have felt entitled to alter to fit their requirements, including shortening films to maximize the number of screenings and cutting out material the exhibitor deemed inappropriate. Therefore, research must be done to find shooting scripts, directors' notes, and other preproduction materials to ensure the restoration is as complete as possible.

Established in 1990 by Martin Scorsese, the Film Foundation helps to conserve motion picture history by supporting preservation and restoration projects at film archives. The foundation has helped save more than 560 motion pictures. It prioritizes funding each year according to physical urgency. Also taken into account is the significance of a project, whether the film is an important work of a writer, actor, or director, or a technical first, or whether it approaches some social issue ahead of its time.

At its core, the Film Foundation represents a natural progression for Scorsese, arguably the world's greatest film enthusiast. Margaret Bodde, a film producer and executive director of the Film Foundation, says, "With Marty, what is so remarkable is his dedication to preservation and film as culture and an art form. He doesn't do it as an obligation; he does it because he wants future generations to be as inspired by film as he was."

Scorsese's storied career gained its inspiration from the numerous films he viewed growing up in Manhattan's Little Italy. One film that inspired Scorsese with a model for how to shoot the fight sequences in his 1980 film *Raging Bull* was *The Red Shoes* (1948), the ballet-centered masterpiece created by the powerhouse British directing team of Michael Powell and Emeric Pressburger. The Film Foundation funded its restoration in 2006, the first fully digital restoration with which it was involved.

Working from the original film negatives, preservationists found that tiny imperfections from the original film development had been exacerbated by time. In addition, much of the film had shrunk. Colors flickered, became mottled, and showed other types of distortion. The film also showed red, blue, and green specks throughout. Worst of all, mold had damaged the negatives.

After the film underwent an extensive cleaning process, it was digitized: 579,000 individual frames had to be scanned. Colors were reregistered, scratches smoothed, flecks removed, and color inconsistencies addressed. Last, a new filmstrip was produced.

The rapid shift from photochemical to digital production has raised concerns. Bodde says, "If a film is born digital, there should be a film output" because of the possibility of data corruption or the unavailability of playback mechanisms. The Film Foundation is working with archivists, technologists, and preservationists to ensure that photochemical preservation continues.

The foundation also offers an interdisciplinary curriculum to help develop visual literacy and film knowledge. This curriculum, The Story of Movies, has been embraced by well over thirty thousand schools. All of this effort works to ensure that future generations know the wonder of watching Moira Shearer move through the vivid, Technicolor dreamscapes of *The Red Shoes* and many other treasures of our film heritage.

Now let's look at some sample inference questions you could potentially encounter after a full-length passage such as this.

1. Based on the information in the first paragraph (lines 1-11), it can be reasonably inferred that after 1950, the type of nitrate on which films were recorded was:

   A. unlikely to shrink or break.
   B. fire resistant.
   C. no longer available.
   D. increasingly popular.

As is true for any question, you want to begin by identifying the key words that tell you the specific focus of the question – in this case, "nitrate."

Where does the passage talk about nitrate? The word first appears in the sentence beginning in line 7, and it continues to appear in the following sentence as well. So it makes sense to read from line 7 to the end of the paragraph.

What information do we get from the sentence beginning in line 7? Until 1950, the (cellulose) nitrate on which films were recorded was flammable. If the nitrate **was** flammable **until** 1950, that means it was **not** flammable **after** 1950. In other words, it was "fire resistant" after 1950. So the answer is (B).

That answer is confirmed by the following sentence, which states that type of nitrate introduced after 1950 *solved the flammability problem* and essentially rephrases the correct answer.

Let's do another one:

2. It is reasonable to infer that prior to 2006, the Film Foundation:

   F. focused exclusively on British films.
   G. was directed by the team of Michael Powell and Emeric Pressburger.
   H. had never undertaken a fully digital restoration.
   J. only restored films that had influenced Martin Scorsese's work.

Although this question does not provide a specific line reference, it does provide information that is relatively straightforward to locate; you simply have to scan the passage for the date *2006*.

If you happen to remember where it appears, you're in luck. If, on the other hand, you don't remember and start reading through the passage carefully from the beginning, you have the potential to waste an enormous amount of time. You therefore need to think strategically. If you truly have no idea where the date is located, you can take your finger and run it down the edge of the passage, scanning each line and making sure not to waste time by stopping and reading.

If you remember seeing the date near the top of the right-hand column, you can be a bit more strategic and start by scanning from the top of that column.

Alternately, you can try skimming the first and last sentence of each paragraph because that is where important information is most likely to be located. In this case, the strategy will work – the date happens to be located in the last sentence of the paragraph in lines 54-62. (That said, scanning first and last sentences is by no means a consistently reliable strategy when a question asks about a detail that you do not remember at all.)

Having found the date in line 61, you now want to reread the entire sentence in which it appears. But since the sentence doesn't make a huge amount of sense on its own, it's a good idea to back up and read the previous sentence as well. In this case, it's not actually necessary to answer the question, but it's helpful for context.

> *One film that inspired Scorsese with a model for how to shoot the fight sequences in his 1980 film* Raging Bull *was* The Red Shoes *(1948), the ballet-centered masterpiece created by the powerhouse British directing team of Michael Powell and Emeric Pressburger. The Film Foundation funded its restoration in 2006, the first fully digital restoration with which it was involved.*

Now let's consider what the passage tells us about 2006: that was the year when the Film Foundation performed its **first** digital restoration. **Statements that indicate when particular events or situations occurred for the first time are excellent candidates for inference questions. By definition, the events discussed could not have occurred before the date provided and must have occurred at that time (and after).** Here, the fact that the Film Foundation's first digital restoration occurred in 2006 directly implies that it had never carried out a digital restoration before that time. The answer must therefore be (H).

Notice that the incorrect answers are all based on words and phrases that appear in the passage. If you do not carefully consider what the question is asking and instead jump to look for an answer containing words from the passage, you are likely to get fooled. Take (G), for example. The phrase *British directing team of Michael Powell and Emeric Pressburger* does in fact appear in the passage; however, it refers to the movie *The Red Shoes* and has nothing to do with the Film Foundation. It is *a* right answer – it just isn't *the* right answer to this particular question.

Now let's look at an inference question that isn't related to dates:

3. The passage suggests that Moira Shearer was:

    A. the person responsible for restoring *The Red Shoes*.
    B. the developer of The Story of Movies curriculum.
    C. an actress in a film directed by Martin Scorsese.
    D. an actress in a film restored by the Film Foundation.

Again, the primary difficulty in this question involves locating the necessary information.

If you truly have no idea where the name is located, you can again take your finger and run it down the edge of the passage, searching for the words *Moira Shearer*. If you remember seeing the name somewhere toward the end of the passage, you can start a few paragraphs from the end.

Again, skimming the first and last sentence of each paragraph happens to work here – the name is located in the last sentence of the passage. Once you've located it (line 91), you can start thinking about the answer. The passage describes Shearer as *mov[ing] through the vivid, Technicolor dreamscapes of The Red Shoes*, indicating that she was either a character in the film or an actress. That eliminates (A) and (B).

The question now becomes how to choose between (C) and (D). In this case, it is very helpful to back up and think about the big picture – more helpful, in fact, than focusing exclusively on the last paragraph. The whole last part of that paragraph, beginning in line 54, describes the Film Foundation's restoration of *The Red Shoes*. If you happen to recall that piece of information, you'll know right away that (D) is correct.

If you feel the need to check out (C), you can still get the right answer, but you'll waste a lot of time in the process. You'll have to go all the way back up to lines 59-60, which state that Michael Powell and Emeric Pressburger – not Martin Scorsese – directed *The Red Shoes*.

You may also encounter inference questions that are closer to main-point or primary-purpose questions – that is, they ask you to make a generalization about a larger idea or theme based on specific information in the passage.

For example, you could see a question that looks like this:

> 4. Information provided in lines 1-33 suggests that the process of preserving and restoring films is:
>
>   F. complex and challenging.
>   G. undergone by the majority of films.
>   H. responsible for preserving 90 percent of films.
>   J. rarely successful.

There are multiple lines that support the correct answer to this question. The author states that film material is *flammable and highly susceptible to deterioration*, and that *Actual restoration is a further, complicated step that many films will never undergo. Restoring celluloid films is a costly, time-consuming process.* Although those lines do not use the actual words "complex" and "challenging," they contain synonyms (e.g., *time-consuming*) that explicitly convey that idea.

(G) is incorrect because the passage states that *many films will never undergo [restoration]*, and (H) is incorrect because the passage indicates that 90 percent of films made before 1950 *have been lost*. Although the figure 90 percent is mentioned, it has nothing whatsoever to do with the question.

Be careful with (J): it might seem reasonable to assume that since restoring films is so difficult, it doesn't have a high success rate, but the passage says absolutely nothing about how successful or unsuccessful the process is. If there is no specific wording to directly support an answer, that answer is not correct. You can't make the leap based only on what seems sort of reasonable to you.

Extended Reasoning

One less common type of inference question asks you to move beyond the passage itself and identify whether information in the passage supports or weakens an idea/example presented in the question. In order to answer this type of question successfully, you must be able to make a generalization based on the specific wording of the passage and then apply it to a new situation. (For *Official Guide, 2018* examples, see #1 and #7 on p. 369.)

For example, again using the "Film Foundation" passage on p. 86, you could encounter the following question:

> 5. Based on the passage, which of the following films would be most likely to receive priority funding from the Film Foundation?
>
> A. a science fiction movie from the 1930s that premiered a then-impressive special effect.
> B. a documentary based on the life of a former United States President.
> C. a film adapted from a novel by a best-selling author.
> D. a film in which a famous actress made a cameo appearance.

Although the passage does not specifically mention any of these types of films, it does discuss the Film Foundation's criteria for "priority funding." If you scan the passage, you'll find the phrase *prioritizes funding* in line 39.

Here, you need to be a little careful. The information after the key phrase states that the Foundation *prioritizes funding each year according to physical urgency*. Unfortunately, no answer corresponds to that idea.

The transition *also* at the beginning of the next sentence is a signal to keep reading. If you do so, you'll find that factors including *the significance of a project, whether the film is an important work of a writer, actor, or director, or a technical first, or whether it approaches some social issue ahead of its time* are also considered.

So basically, priority is given to films that have some sort of artistically, cultural, or technical distinction, or that did something important for the first time. That's the general idea, and the correct answer must provide an example consistent with it.

The only answer that fits is (A): a film that "premiered" an "impressive" special effect (even if it was only impressive by 1930s standards) would be consistent with that requirement.

9 Tone and Attitude

....

Questions about tone and attitude test what the author/narrator or another figure in the passage thinks about a particular person or situation. Some of these questions ask about short sections of the passage, while others will ask you to consider the passage as a whole. This question type appears on virtually every test, but usually not more than once or twice.

Playing Positive and Negative

As a general rule, the easiest way to answer tone/attitude questions is to start by determining whether the relevant figure's tone or attitude is positive or negative. If it is positive, you can automatically eliminate any negative answer(s) and vice versa. Sometimes, you will be left with the correct answer on that basis alone.

Other times, however, you will not be quite so fortunate and will need to consider several answers carefully in order to determine which one is best supported by the passage. If the passage does not contain a synonym for the correct answer choice, it will include specific words and/or phrases that directly convey or suggest the attitude indicated in the right answer. In this sense, attitude questions also test vocabulary, both in the passage and in the answer choices.

The chart on the following page shows some answer choices that have appeared on previous ACTs, grouped by positive, negative, and neutral. Because answer choices to tone and attitude questions are frequently recycled from test to test, you should make sure to familiarize yourself with any words whose definitions you are uncertain of.

Positive	Negative	Neutral
Accepting	Alarmed	Detached
Admiring	Angry	Frank
Amused	Antagonistic	Neutral
Appreciative	Bashful	
Awe	Concerned	
Calming	Condescending	
Carefree	Confused	
Commendable	Critical	
Confident	Cynical	
Delighted	Disapproving	
Determined	Disbelieving	
Dynamic	Discomfort	
Enthusiastic	Disdainful	
Excited	Disrespectful	
Fascinated	Dismissive	
Humorous	Exhausted	
Insightful	Guarded	
Inspiring	Impatient	
Intrigued	Inhibited	
Mesmerizing	Ironic	
Peaceful	Pity	
Proud	Overwhelmed	
Respectful	Questioning	
Reverent	Resigned	
Spirited	Risky	
Worshipful	Scornful	
	Senseless	
	Skeptical	
	Uncertain	
	Uncomfortable	
	Undesirable	
	Uneasy	
	Unsatisfying	
	Unsettling	

Example #1

The composer Joseph Bertolozzi, bearing a
meditative look, stood with his feet apart in front of
a door frame inside the Eiffel Tower. Then, 187 feet
above the Champs de Mars garden, he pulled
5   a latex mallet from his tool bag and hit the frame
hard, and then softer, with agility and rhythm.

"That one was beautiful!" said Paul Kozel, a
sound engineer, who recorded the dull thuds.
10

Mr. Bertolozzi, who lives in Beacon, N.Y., is
in Paris harvesting sounds for what he calls a
"public art installation," a musical project that has
taken him, Mr. Kozel and a team of seven to one of
15   the most visited monuments in the world.

His mission is to "play the Eiffel Tower" by
striking its surfaces, collecting sounds through a
microphone and using them as samples for an hour-
20   long composition called "Tower Music." He
eventually hopes for a live, on-site performance of
the work to celebrate the tower's 125th
anniversary next year. "I'm exhilarated to be here,"
Mr. Bertolozzi said, just before striking a wall with
25   a sheepskin-padded log hanging from a leather
strap. "I've been planning this for so long."

1. Based on the fourth paragraph (lines 17-
    26), Joseph Bertolozzi's attitude toward
    "playing" the Eiffel Tower is one of:

    A. curiosity and bewilderment.
    B. uneasiness and uncertainty.
    C. excitement and enthusiasm.
    D. indifference and annoyance.

Solution: In line 23, Bertolozzi states that he is *exhilarated* by the prospect of "playing" the
Eiffel Tower, and that *[He's] been planning this for so long*, clearly indicating that he has an
extremely positive attitude. *Exhilarated* is a synonym for "excitement and enthusiasm,"
making (C) correct.

If you want to play process of elimination and think about the question in terms of
positive/negative, all of the other answer choices contain at least one negative word, making
(C) the only possible answer.

Example #2

During the years I spent in the company of Alexander Graham Bell, at work on his biography, I often wondered what the inventor of the world's most important acoustical device—the telephone — might
5 have sounded like.

Born in Scotland in 1847, Bell, at different periods of his life, lived in England, then Canada and, later, the Eastern Seaboard of the United States. His favorite
10 refuge was Cape Breton Island, Nova Scotia, where he spent the summers from the mid-1880s on. In his day, 85 percent of the population there conversed in Gaelic. Did Bell speak with a Scottish burr? What was the pitch and depth of the voice with which he loved to
15 belt out ballads and music hall songs?

Someone who knew that voice was his grand-daughter, Mabel Grosvenor, a noted Washington, D.C. pediatrician who retired in 1966. In 2004, I met with
20 Dr. Mabel, as she was known in the family, when she was 99 years old—clearheaded, dignified and a bit fierce. I inquired whether her grandfather had an accent. "He sounded," she said firmly, "like you." As a British-born immigrant to Canada, my accent is BBC
25 English with a Canadian overlay: It made instant sense to me that I would share intonations and pronunciations with a man raised in Edinburgh who had resided in North America from the age of 23. When Dr. Mabel died in 2006, the last direct link with the inventor was
30 gone.

2. Information in the first and second paragraphs (lines 1-15) indicates that the author's attitude toward Alexander Graham Bell's voice was one of:

F. dismay.
G. amusement.
H. scorn.
J. curiosity.

Solution: The information you need to answer this question can be found in two places: the first paragraph, in which the author states that she *often wondered* about what Bell's voice sounded like; and at the end of the second paragraph, which ends with two consecutive questions about the accent and cadence of Bell's speech. Those two places clearly indicate that the author was "curious" about Bell's voice – she wanted to know more about it and spent time wondering what specific features might characterize it. In addition, the word *wondered* by definition suggests curiosity.

If you wanted to play positive/negative, you could see that the author's attitude is somewhat positive (she probably wouldn't want to know more about Bell's voice unless she found it interesting) and eliminate (F) and (H) on that basis. You could also eliminate (G) because there is nothing in the passage to indicate that the author was "amused" by Bell's voice.

Example #3

"Come, come!" my mother urged us forward. It
was the custom to greet the old. "Deborah!" my mother
urged. Deborah stepped forward and took Ultima's
withered hand.

5   "Buenos dias, Grande," she smiled. She even
bowed slightly. Then she pulled Theresa forward and
told her to greet la Grande. My mother beamed.
Deborah's good manners surprised her, but they made
her happy, because a family was judged by its
10   manners.

"What beautiful daughters you have raised,"
Ultima nodded to my mother. Nothing could have
pleased my mother more. She looked proudly at my
father who stood leaning against the truck, watching
15   and judging the introductions.

"Antonio," he said simply. I stepped forward and
took Ultima's hand. I looked up into her clear brown
eyes and shivered. Her face was old and wrinkled, but
her eyes were clear and sparkling, like the eyes of a
20   young child.

"Antonio, she smiled. She took my hand, and I felt
the power of a whirlwind sweep around me. Her eyes
swept the surrounding hills and through them I saw for
the first time the wild beauty of our hills and the magic
25   of the green river. My nostrils quivered as I felt the
song of the mockingbirds and the drone of the
grasshoppers mingle with the pulse of the earth. The
four directions of the llano met in me, and the white sun
shone on my soul. The granules of sand at my feet and
30   the sun and sky above me seemed to dissolve into one
strange complete being.

A cry came to my throat, and I wanted to shout it
and run in the beauty I had found.

3.   In the fifth paragraph and sixth paragraphs
      (lines 22-34), Antonio reacts to Ultima with:

      A. scorn and indifference.
      B. awe and amazement.
      C. bashfulness and reluctance.
      D. calm and resignation.

Solution: The easiest way to approach this question is to play positive/negative. Antonio's reaction to Ultima is very clearly positive: he sees the *wild beauty of the hills and the magic of the green river*, and *the white sun shone on [his] soul*. That eliminates (A) and (C), which are clearly negative. In (D), "calm" could fit, but look at the other half of the answer: "resignation" indicates passive acceptance, usually of a bad situation, and that's not what's happening here. In fact, Antonio wants to *shout it and run in the beauty [he] had found*. So (D) doesn't work either. That leaves (B), which captures the intense sense of wonder Antonio feels upon meeting Ultima.

Now let's look at a full-length passage.

"A finite universe"—that's the phrase that Jim Kuhn uses to describe the surviving early quartos of Shakespeare's plays. It evokes something that seems more expansive and dynamic than the estimated 777 paperback-sized volumes that, for the last four hundred years, have physically carried our most direct evidence of the Bard's work. It also begins to suggest the appeal of those volumes in aggregate: There is an end to their universe, the texts that define it can be collected, and that collection, completed.

Five years ago, Kuhn, then head of collection information services at the Folger Shakespeare Library, helped to prototype just such a collection: a digital repository capable of bringing together in one location the sparse and geographically scattered universe of these rare Shakespeare texts. The project, which was led by the Folger and the University of Oxford, involved librarians, curators, computer scientists, educators, and interns from scholarly institutions on both sides of the Atlantic.

As a proof of concept, they tackled the thirty-two early copies of *Hamlet* held by the participating libraries (the Folger, the British Library, the Bodleian Library at Oxford, the Huntington Library, the National Library of Scotland, and the University of Edinburgh Library). Sixteen months spent gathering cover-to-cover digital images, producing transcriptions, and developing an online interface resulted, in November of 2009, in the Shakespeare Quartos Archive, which boasts the most comprehensive collection of early Hamlets available and is setting an example for newer literary archives such as the recently announced Shelley–Godwin Archive.

Among Shakespeare's works, *Hamlet* is an obvious choice for such an endeavor, not only because of the play's iconic status in literary and popular culture, but because many perplexities surround its textual transmission. "*Hamlet* goes from the stage to the printed page at one point or another," says Steven Galbraith, another former member of the SQA's Folger team; "but the printed page is, materially, what survives for us." We don't have an authorial manuscript (of *Hamlet* or any of the Bard's works) against which to judge those pages, and, as it turns out, we don't have an unassailably stable *Hamlet* in any form: We have *Hamlets*, plural—a circumstance that becomes amply clear when one turns to the surviving quartos themselves. Look closely enough, and not just every edition, but every copy differs from every other.

Helping readers get a good look at these quartos is where the SQA excels. Partnering with yet another scholarly institution (the Maryland Institute for Technology in the Humanities, which is part of the University of Maryland, College Park), the SQA team developed a web-based interface and set of digital tools designed for close, almost microscopic, comparative analysis. Among a number of other features, one can execute word searches on the texts, superimpose and adjust the transparency of page images, and run a difference algorithm that immediately highlights every inconsistency—including printers' marks, marginal notations, and other paratextual matter—between any two of the archive's scrupulously executed transcriptions. Armed with these tools, the "originals" can begin to look like a dense patchwork of inconsistency—*Hamlet*, hopelessly at odds with itself.

Galbraith, a curator by trade, has another perspective on the body of evidence that the SQA offers up, one that looks beyond the *Hamlet* texts themselves, to their value as archaeological specimens. "Every book has its own story," he says, "and using the SQA with a critical eye, you can really begin to see that. There are differences in bindings, different people have owned them and marked them up, used them in different ways." And the bigger question, he adds, the one to which all these differences lead, is one of provenance: "Where has this book been for the last four hundred years?" Tracing the hand or characteristic markings of some previous reader through the text, focusing on the passages or words that he or she focused on, identifying the binder or the most worn pages, one can begin to piece together the trajectories of these individual books through history and how they were used.

The SQA's collection of high-resolution and transcribed *Hamlets* may, with some clever detective work, prove a boon to literary scholars and bibliographers. But, as both Kuhn and Galbraith point out, the archive also helps to raise and answer questions touching on digitization efforts beyond Shakespeare: What do you do when the imaging and transcription are done? What can you do with the texts now that you couldn't do before? Neither the content of the plays—the lines, words, punctuation marks, paratextual matter, marginalia—nor the images of their physical medium necessarily suggest all of the uses to which the data might be put. Making the texts accessible, and, what is more important, accessible as data, opens them up to modes of analysis and creativity beyond those traditionally associated with the humanities. "The goal," says Galbraith, "is to release that data and let the scholars, directors, and artists, or whoever is coming to the quartos, do their work with them in whatever way, for whatever reason." One wonders what a statistician, digital artist, or data visualization expert might find in the SQA.

1. Which of the following best characterizes the author's attitude toward archive he discusses in the passage?

   A. He regards it critically because it will not allow scholars to compile a definitive version of *Hamlet*.
   B. He believes that it is likely to fail because it will only appeal to a small number of specialists.
   C. He views it with appreciation because it will offer insights to Shakespeare scholars as well as experts in other fields.
   D. He welcomes it as a tool that fully explains the significance of marginalia and paratextual matters in Shakespeare's plays.

At first glance, a question like this might seem quite complex – the answer choices are all lengthy and jam-packed with information – and perhaps a bit overwhelming. It's important, however, that you not give into that initial sense of panic and start to read frantically back through the passage. Give yourself a moment to worry; then, pull yourself together and think about it logically.

The first thing to notice is that the answer choices contain two negative options, (A) and (B), and two positive options, (C) and (D). As a result, your first goal is to determine whether the author's attitude is positive or negative. If you understood the passage well, you can probably figure out that since the author spends a lot of time discussing all the ways in which the archive will help people better understand *Hamlet*, his attitude is positive. The passage is also about integrating technology into a field that traditionally hasn't had much to do with computers – almost always a good thing for the ACT.

If you do need to look back at the passage, though, you want to focus on the place where the author's attitude usually comes through most clearly: the conclusion. As you reread it, make sure to look out for words that are clearly positive or negative. What does it tell you? That the archive is a *boon to literary scholars and bibliographers*, that it *makes the texts accessible* and *opens them up to new modes of analysis and creativity*. That's pretty positive, so eliminate (A) and (B).

Now the question becomes *why* the author's attitude is positive. The key again is in the conclusion, which tells you that the archive will open up Shakespeare's work to a variety of experts (*scholars, directors, artists*), so (C) is correct. (D) states the correct attitude but follows it with complicated-sounding details that are re-presented in a false context: the passage indicates that neither *marginalia [nor] paratextual matters...suggest all the uses to which data might be put*. In other words, these things are of limited use. That's exactly the opposite of what (D) says.

10 Point of View

. . . .

Questions asking about point of view are most likely to appear in conjunction with Prose Fiction and Humanities (memoir) passages, but they do sometimes accompany other passage types as well. In general, however, you should go out of your way to pay attention to point of view whenever you read a Prose Fiction passage; usually, the first question will ask about the perspective from which the passage is written.

ACT Reading passages are generally written from two points of view:

First-person passages are written from the narrator's point of view and are characterized by the use of the first-person pronoun *I*. Prose Fiction passages written in the first person are narrated from the point of view of the protagonist, a fictional character, whereas Humanities passages written in the first person are narrated from the point of view of the author him- or herself. Stylistically, however, the two are often indistinguishable.

For example, consider the following two passages.

Passage #1

In those days, cheap apartments were almost impossible to find in Manhattan, so I had to move to Brooklyn. This was in 1947, and one of the pleasant features of that summer which I so vividly remember
5 was the weather, which was sunny and mild, flower-fragrant, almost as if the days had been arrested in a seemingly perpetual springtime. I was grateful for that if for nothing else, since my youth, I felt, was at its lowest ebb.

10 At twenty-two, struggling to become some kind of writer, I found that the creative heat which at eighteen had nearly consumed me with its gorgeous, relentless flame had flickered out to a dim pilot light registering little more than a token glow in my breast,
15 or wherever my hungriest aspirations once resided. It was not that I no longer wanted to write. I still yearned passionately to produce the novel which had been for so long captive in my brain. It was only that, having written down the first few fine paragraphs, I
20 could not produce any others, or—to approximate Gertrude Stein's remark about a lesser writer of the Lost Generation—I had the syrup but it wouldn't pour. To make matters worse, I was out of a job and had very little money and was self-exiled to Flatbush.

Passage #2

When Neil Baldwin of the National Book Foundation called to inquire if I would agree to be one of the fiction judges for the 2000 National Book Awards, I responded with an immediate
5 and enthusiastic yes. It was a great honor. An opportunity to influence the course of American letters and uphold the standard of art. Under the enthusiasm a certain trepidation gnawed at me: Would I be able to do the job, and do it well?
10 And what about the novel I was halfway through writing? But I blithely shrugged it off.

Until the 300-plus volumes we were to judge showed up at my doorstep.

To keep up with the grueling schedule the
15 judges had been set, I read nonstop, pausing only to jot down notes and questions before picking up a new book. I'd immerse myself in the worlds of the novels until words ran together. When I closed a book, sometimes it took me a moment
20 to remember where I was. It was a reading experience unlike any I'd ever undertaken, even during graduate school at Berkeley.

The passage on the left-hand side is excerpted from William Styron's novel *Sophie's Choice* (you might have seen the movie with Meryl Streep), while the passage on the right is taken from a *New York Times* article, "Writers on Writing: New Insights into the Novel." If you were to encounter these excerpts out of context, however, you would have no way of knowing for certain which one was fiction and which one was non-fiction. In both cases, the narrators also employ a perspective typical of ACT Reading passages – they are writing after the events described in the passage have already occurred, and reflecting on the experience of those events. When characters described in Prose Fiction passages are either children or adolescents, the passages are **nearly always written from the perspective of an adult looking back on a memorable experience – often one from their youth**. The fact that passages are written in the **past tense** indicates that the events they describe have already ended. In addition, people usually do not truly understand the significance of their childhood or young-adult experiences until long after those experiences have occurred.

This is important to recognize because the first question accompanying Prose Fiction passages often asks about the point of view from which the passage is written. In general, answers stating that the passage is written from a child's perspective can be eliminated, while those stating that it is written from that of an adult should be considered first. Furthermore, when a passage is written in the past tense, you can also assume that answers indicating that the situation described in the passage is still occurring are incorrect.

Third-person passages are written from an **objective point of view** – that is, the narrator does not directly participate in the action, and people are referred to as *he* or *she*, not *I*. Although you may have studied different types of third-person narrators in school (e.g., fully omniscient, partially omniscient), the ACT is exceedingly unlikely to test this terminology directly. Rather, the test is focused on gauging your understanding of whether narrators are directly involved in the action. As a general rule, third-person narrators are **interested observers** – they find the subject of the passage engaging, but their personal involvement is limited. Social Science and Natural Science passages are usually written from this perspective, and it is common in Prose Fiction and Humanities as well. For example, the author of a passage about jazz is likely to be a person who has a serious interest in jazz but is not actually a jazz musician.

When you think about the framework of the ACT, this makes perfect sense: virtually all third-person Social Science, Humanities, and Natural Science passages are **journalistic**. That is, they are drawn from articles published in moderately serious newspapers, magazines, and non-fiction books – works written for non-expert readers who are interested in a variety of topics. The author's job is therefore to explain the essentials of the topic to the audience, avoiding any insider terminology or references likely to be unfamiliar to the general public.

For example, consider the introduction to the "Shakespeare" passage we've looked at before:

> "A finite universe"—that's the phrase that Jim Kuhn uses
> to describe the surviving early quartos of Shakespeare's plays.
> It evokes something that seems more expansive and dynamic
> than the estimated 777 paperback-sized volumes that, for the
> last four hundred years, have physically carried our most direct
> evidence of the Bard's work. It also begins to suggest the
> appeal of those volumes in aggregate: There is an end to their
> universe, the texts that define it can be collected, and that
> collection, completed.

The author's style is typical of most ACT Humanities/Social Science passages. The author clearly suggests his positive attitude toward the subject through phrases like *more expansive and dynamic* and *It begins to suggest the <u>appeal</u> of those volumes*, but there is also nothing to suggest that the author has a direct stake in the subject. The focus is on Shakespeare's quartos, and what they represent; the author himself indicates no involvement in the subject other than the fact that he is writing about it.

Occasionally, a passage may include more than one type of narration. For example, consider the beginning of the "Alexander Graham Bell" passage on p. 94.

There is a shift in point of view between the two paragraphs: in the first paragraph, the author employs a first-person perspective, as indicated by the repeated use of the word *I*. In the second paragraph, however, she changes direction and focuses on Alexander Graham Bell, beginning a third-person narration (note the repetition of words *he* and *his*).

When you do an initial read-through of a passage, you should always make sure to mark the spot where this type of shift in point of view occurs. The paragraph where the new point of view is introduced will mark the beginning of a new section; moreover, that spot is an excellent candidate for a paragraph-function question.

Points of view other than first person (singular) and third person are rare – in general as well as on the ACT – but do appear occasionally. A **first person plural** narration is characterized by the use of the pronouns *we*, *our*, and *us*. For example, consider this excerpt from a recent newspaper editorial:

> The bottom line is very simple: As parents, **we** always put our children's interests first. **We** wake up every morning and go to bed every night worrying about their well-being and their futures. And when **we** make decisions about our kids' health, we rely on doctors and experts who can give **us** accurate information based on sound science. **Our** leaders in Washington should do the same.

A **second person** narration is characterized by the use of the pronoun *you* – that is, the author addresses the reader directly.

> Half the job of a working writer is to seek and maintain his own affinities. **You've** got to know where to lay your empathy and why. And **you've** got to know how to recognize the kind of material that releases your imagination. **You** don't always find those things in other novelists: often, indeed, it will be the artist in the next field, the craftsman, the expert, the sportsman, the hero in another line, who will pump fresh air into the recesses of **your** talent.

Both of these points of view are used by authors who are attempting to draw their readers in and establish a connection to them. They are also used by authors who are seeking to persuade their readers, or urge them toward a particular course of action. If one of these points of view appears in conjunction with an answer choice that involves persuading or urging, that answer is likely to be correct.

11 Paired Passages

Paired passages are the most recent addition to the ACT Reading Test. While both passages in a paired set always discuss the same topic, the exact relationship between them varies. Although the authors could disagree, released exams suggest that paired passages are more likely to focus on different aspects of an idea or situation, or to use one passage to illustrate an idea presented in the other. The authors may also agree on some ideas and disagree on others. Even if that is the case, you should pay close attention to what the authors would agree on because you are likely to see a question asking just that.

If the two passages do present similar ideas, they are likely to contain differences in style, tone, or point of view. For example, one passage might be written in the third person while the other is written in the first person. Alternately, the tone of one passage might be slightly negative while the tone of the other passage is slightly positive. You should always look out for these types of differences since they are excellent fodder for relationship questions.

While paired passages might seem like a lot to manage, you should keep in mind that most of questions accompanying paired passages ask about one passage only. You can expect to see only three questions that ask about the relationship between the two passages. As a result, you can generally treat paired passages just as you would any other passages.

Furthermore, if you grasp the basic relationship between the passages, you can often use your big-picture knowledge to determine answers quickly. And in some cases, questions that appear to ask about both passages can actually be answered using only one passage.

In general, your goal should be to deal with the smallest possible amount of information at any given time. The more work you do upfront, the less work you'll need to do on the questions. To that end, you may find the following "formula" helpful:

1. Read Passage A: write main point and tone (positive/negative/neutral).
2. Answer Passage A questions.
3. Read Passage B: write main point, tone, relationship to Passage A (e.g., agree, disagree, example).
4. Answer Passage B questions.
5. Answer Passage A vs. Passage B relationship questions.

Remember that the main point of both passages is usually located in one of two key places: the end of the introduction and the end of the conclusion. **In addition, the easiest way to determine the relationship between them is usually to focus on the end of the first passage and the beginning of the second – the place where the passages are juxtaposed most directly.** On the next page, we're going to look at an example.

Passage A

Happiness – you know it when you see it, but it's hard to define. You might call it a sense of well-being, of optimism or of meaningfulness in life, although those could also be treated as separate entities. But whatever happiness is, we know that we want it, and that it is just somehow good.

We also know that we don't always have control over our happiness. Research suggests that genetics may play a big role in our normal level of subjective well-being, so some of us may start out at a disadvantage. On top of that, between unexpected tragedies and daily habitual stress, environmental factors can bring down mood and dry up our thirst for living. Being able to manage the emotional ups and downs is important for both body and mind, said Laura Kubzansky, professor of social and behavioral sciences at Harvard School of Public Health. "For physical health, it's not so much happiness per se, but this ability to regulate and have a sense of purpose and meaning," Kubzansky says. Many scientific studies, including some by Kubzansky, have found a connection between psychological and physical well-being.

A 2012 review of more than 200 studies found a connection between positive psychological attributes, such as happiness, optimism and life satisfaction, and a lowered risk of cardiovascular disease. Kubzansky and other Harvard School of Public Health researchers published these findings in the journal *Psychological Bulletin*.

It's not as simple as "you must be happy to prevent heart attacks," of course. If you have a good sense of well-being, it's easier to maintain good habits: Exercising, eating a balanced diet and getting enough sleep, researchers say. People who have an optimistic mindset may be more likely to engage in healthy behaviors because they perceive them as helpful in achieving their goals, Kubzansky said.

For now these studies can only show associations; they do not provide hard evidence of cause and effect. But some researchers speculate that positive mental states do have a direct effect on the body, perhaps by reducing damaging physical processes.

Passage B

In reality, there is no clear-cut answer yet on whether being upbeat can keep you healthy or cure anything. For some diseases, which may build over decades, the relationship between patients' attitudes and their prognosis is dubious at best. For other diseases, though, the scientific outlook is sunnier. There's evidence that mood can predict whether someone who has had one heart attack will have another. Little research has been done on the biological basis of positive thinking as a therapeutic treatment for illness, but scientists know the brain and the immune system communicate. Given that scientists also know the immune system plays a role in inflammation of the arteries, which can play a role in heart attacks, it's reasonable to think that heart attacks could be tied back to things going on in the brain. However, when researchers tried to intercede and treat depression among heart attack patients, they found the patient's moods improved, but the rates of second heart attack didn't. Ironically the most evidence for emotion affecting health actually favors negative emotions, not positive ones. For instance, we know anger and depression are correlated with having a second heart attack; however, what's unproven is whether being positive can reduce the risk.

Another way emotion could affect health, even for complicated illnesses such as cancer, is by affecting the patient's willingness to stick to the treatment plan. "It could be an indirect effect," said Anne Harrington, chair of Harvard University's history of science program and author of *The Cure Within: A History of Mind-Body Medicine*. If a person is positive, he or she is more likely to show up for all the treatments, to have a better diet, to exercise. And if you're deeply depressed you sleep badly and that's bad for your health.

What do we have in terms of main point and tone?

Passage A

Main point: happiness = probably good f/health

Tone: slightly positive, cautiously optimistic

Passage B

Main point: Not sure if happiness = health

Tone: slightly negative, skeptical

Relationship: Disagree...and agree

The author of Passage A is a bit more receptive toward the idea that happiness could have a positive effect on people's health. In contrast, the author of Passage B stresses that if emotions do affect health, it's more likely the case for negative emotions.

That said, the authors of both passages *agree* that the data isn't exactly clear: happiness could have a direct impact on a person's health, or those two things could just be correlated. That information would become very important if you encountered the following question:

> Based on the passages, it can be reasonably inferred that the the authors would most likely agree that the effects of happiness on well-being:
>
> **A.** are more apparent today than they were in the past.
> **B.** will require additional research to be fully understood.
> **C.** were conclusively demonstrated by Laura Kubzansky in 2012.
> **D.** are stronger than the effects of negative emotions on illness.

At first glance, these questions appear to ask about the entirety of both passages. As a result, it might seem as if the answer could be anywhere. You might even be tempted to starting rereading both passages from the beginning. In reality, however, the answers can be determined from a few key lines at the end of Passage A and the beginning of Passage B.

End of Passage A:

> *For now these studies [about the effects of happiness on health] can only show associations; they do not provide hard evidence of cause and effect. But some researchers speculate that positive mental states do have a direct effect on the body, perhaps by reducing damaging physical processes.* (lines 40-44)

Beginning of Passage B:

> *In reality, there is no clear-cut answer yet on whether being upbeat can keep you healthy or cure anything.* (lines 46-48)

The phrases *for now* in Passage A and *no clear-cut answer yet* in Passage B indicate that as research currently stands, scientists do not have enough information to determine whether there is a direct link between happiness and health. In other words, more research is needed. And that is what (B) says.

Agreement questions can also be asked much more simply:

> A similarity between the passages is that they both:
>
> **A.** describe the ways in which positive thinking is an essential component of a healthy lifestyle.
> **B.** explain how the relationship between the brain and the immune system is affected by a person's mental state.
> **C.** assert that person's level of happiness is the most important factor in predicting illness.
> **D.** suggest that emotions might play a role in people's physical well-being.

Again, this question can be answered with only a few key pieces of information. Because it's a big-picture question, you don't need to worry about the details of each passage. Instead, focus on the larger ideas that the passages convey.

Start with the main point of Passage A: happiness is probably good for health. (D) is perfectly consistent with that idea, immediately suggesting that it is correct. If you remember enough of the second passage to know that it supports that statement as well, you can choose that answer and move on.

If you're not certain enough about Passage B to choose (D) securely, you need to be more careful. As discussed earlier, the second passage is distinctly more skeptical about the link between happiness and health. If you only consider that fact, you can easily get into trouble.

(D), however, does not state that happiness directly leads to better health, but rather refers to the fact that emotions "might play a role in people's physical well-being." The phrasing is both general and cautious: it leaves ample room for the author of Passage B's skepticism.

Moreover, if you look at the conclusion of Passage B, you'll find that the author does explicitly indicate that emotional state might influence health. (*Another way emotion could affect health, even for complicated illnesses such as cancer, is by affecting the patient's willingness to stick to the treatment plan.*) Despite the obvious skepticism, the author is open to the idea that there might be a connection, albeit an indirect one, between people's emotions and their well-being.

To reiterate, though: When two passages convey similar ideas, you will often be able to answer relationship questions using the information from only one passage. You can consult both passages for reassurance, but you might not actually *need* to spend the time doing so. If the passages agree, then by definition both are making the same point. And if that point appears as an answer choice, then it is very likely to be correct.

Other questions will ask about the relationship between the passages in terms of tone.

Even if there is a difference in tone between the passages, you can assume that most correct answers will be either neutral or somewhat positive/negative. In contrast, incorrect answers will be either too strong emotionally or inconsistent with the serious, moderately formal tone and style that characterize virtually all ACT Reading passages.

For example, consider the following question:

Which statement most accurately compares the tone of each passage?

A. The author of Passage A is dreamy and imaginative, whereas the author of Passage B is harsh and critical.
B. The author of Passage A is optimistic, whereas the author of Passage B is skeptical and cautious.
C. The author of Passage A is humorous and enthusiastic, whereas the author of Passage B is haughty and disdainful.
D. The author of Passage A is dismissive, whereas the author of Passage B is angry and defensive.

If you know that the tone of Passage A is relatively positive and the tone of Passage B is slightly negative, you can probably jump directly to (B). None of the other answers even remotely fits – they all indicate levels of emotion far beyond what either passage contains.

In fact, even if you hadn't read either passage, you could still make a very good educated guess that (B) was correct. The chance that any ACT Social Science passage would be "dreamy," "humorous," "disdainful," "angry" or "defensive" is exceedingly small. Based on that knowledge, you could eliminate (A), (C), and (D) with a fair amount of confidence.

Other relationship questions will ask you to compare either specific portions of each passage, or a specific portion of one passage to the other passage as whole. Even when working with these smaller sections, you may still be able to use the big picture to determine correct and incorrect answers. In addition, you may sometimes also be able to answer these questions using information from only one passage, despite the fact that the questions appear to ask about both passages.

For example:

Compared to Passage A's discussion of the 200 studies reviewed by Laura Kubzansky and other researchers, Passage B's discussion of heart attacks can be described as:

A. more concerned with the therapeutic potential of positive thinking.
B. less concerned with physiological mechanisms involved in producing disease.
C. more concerned with the work of a specific group of scientists.
D. less concerned with the positive relationship between happiness and well-being.

At first glance, this question seems to involve a whole lot of information, and your initial instinct might be to go through each of the answers, checking it against each passage in turn.

It is certainly possible to figure out the right answer eventually that way, but it would also be time consuming and leave a fair amount of room for confusion and second-guessing.

A much more efficient way to determine the answer is to think about each passage as a whole. Again, the author of Passage A believes that happiness probably has a positive effect on health, whereas the author of Passage B is more skeptical toward that idea. Because both passages are fairly short, most of the information in each passage supports its main point.

Using only that information, let's consider the answers again. We're still going to work through them in order, but in a way that will get us to the right answer much more quickly. Remember that although the question mentions both Passage A and Passage B, it is really asking about Passage B, and so that is where you want to direct your attention. In fact, we could start by rephrasing the question in a much simpler manner, e.g., "Describe the discussion of heart attacks in Passage B," or "What does Passage B say about heart attacks that Passage A doesn't?"

To reiterate: you should always start by focusing on the passage the question directly asks about because you may be able to determine the answer from that passage alone.

    A. more concerned with the therapeutic potential of
        positive thinking.
    B. less concerned with physiological mechanisms involved
        in producing disease.
    C. more concerned with the work of a specific group of
        scientists.
    D. less concerned with the positive relationship between
        happiness and well-being.

Be very careful with (A) – it fits with Passage A but directly contradicts Passage B. If you did not read the question carefully, you could easily get mixed up and jump to this answer.

(B) is a classic distractor. It sounds just plausible enough to be true, and you might be tempted to start going through both passages to check it out. We're going to leave it for now, though, because we're looking to see whether there's an option that fits with the big picture.

If you think about what the question is asking, (C) is pretty blatantly wrong. The question states that Passage A refers to "200 studies reviewed by Laura Kubzansky and other researchers." Given that, it's pretty unlikely that Passage B would refer to an even more specific group of scientists. Besides, we're thinking in terms of main ideas, and this answer is much more focused on the details.

(D) fits perfectly. "Less concerned with the positive relationship between happiness and well-being" is another way of saying that the author of Passage B is skeptical about the idea that happiness might contribute to good health. It is not even necessary to consult Passage A.

Note that the "more/less" phrasing of the answer choices has the potential to create confusion because an answer that is negative overall may contain positive words and vice versa (e.g., "less concerned about the positive relationship"). In addition, the word *concerned* is used in a more neutral way than you might be accustomed to – instead of meaning "worried," it means something like "focused on." As a result, you must keep very careful track of just what each answer is actually implying.

Sometimes, however, the big picture will apply to this type of smaller-scale question only indirectly. In some cases, it might not even apply at all.

Consider this version of the question:

> Compared to Passage A's discussion of the 200 studies
> reviewed by Laura Kubzansky and other researchers,
> Passage B's discussion of heart attacks can be described as:
>
> A. more concerned with the therapeutic potential of
> positive thinking.
> B. more concerned with the detrimental effects of emo-
> tions on physical well-being.
> C. less concerned with physiological mechanisms involved
> in producing disease.
> D. less concerned with the relationship between the brain
> and the immune system.

Here, things get a little trickier because there is no answer that directly rephrases the main point of Passage B. If you read very carefully, though, you can work from the assumption that (A) is incorrect and (B) is correct.

Why? Because (A) is positive, and (B) is negative. The other two answers are neutral.

Again, (A) states exactly the opposite of what appears in the passages and can thus be eliminated. (B), however, is consistent with the relationship between the passages. Even if you don't remember the details of Passage B, the phrase "more concerned with the detrimental effects" is key. It indicates that Passage B emphasizes something bad, and that alone should prompt you to pay extra attention.

When you go back and read, you can see that the relevant section of Passage B does in fact present the idea that negative emotions could affect health. (*Ironically the most evidence for emotion affecting health actually favors negative emotions, not positive ones. For instance, we know anger and depression are correlated with having a second heart attack*, lines 64-67.) That may not be the point of the passage, but it's certainly an idea that appears in the passage. Passage A, in contrast, does not mention it at all. The focus is exclusively on positive emotions.

Let's look at another example:

An element of Passage A that is not present in Passage B is a reference to which aspect of research on positive thinking?

A. Effects on heart disease
B. A quotation from a scientific expert
C. Influence of genetics on mood
D. Specific behaviors correlated with positivity

Because the question is phrased somewhat confusingly, we're going to start by simplifying it: "What does Passage A discuss that Passage B doesn't?"

Otherwise, this question is about as straightforward and factual as relationship questions get. In such cases, you will simply have to take the time to check each option against both passages. **It is not a good idea to rely on your memory for details**, although if one answer immediately jumps out at you, you can certainly check it first.

That said, you may be able to use an occasional shortcut – if not to identify correct answers, then at least to eliminate incorrect ones.

Here, for example, (B) is exceptionally easy to check out because any "quotation from a scientific expert" must contain quotation marks along with a specific person's name. You do not really need to read to determine whether these elements are present, but can simply scan for them. As a matter of fact, **if an answer choice refers to quotations, you should check that answer first**. If quotations appear in one passage but not in the other, you can be done in only a few seconds.

In this set of passages, unfortunately, that's not the case. Passage A cites Laura Kubzansky in lines 17-19, and Passage B cites Anne Harrington in lines 72-73.

Now you can work in order, scanning for key words just as you would for any other literal comprehension question.

(A) is incorrect because both authors mention heart attacks, although the author of Passage B spends more time talking about them than the author of Passage A does. Even if you just remember the discussion from Passage B, you can safely eliminate this answer because the question asks only about what is NOT in Passage A.

(C) is correct because only the author of Passage A discusses the influence of genetics on mood. The fast way to determine that this is the answer is to identify "genetics" as the key word and scan each passage for it, running your finger down the page. Note that the word appears close to the beginning of the first passage, so if you start by looking somewhere in the middle, you're likely to miss it.

(D) is incorrect because both passages focus on the correlation between positive thinking about healthful behaviors, and both cite examples such as diet and exercise.

Finally, some relationship questions will ask you to use information from both passages to make an inference or draw a conclusion. Again, while these questions may refer to both passages, you may be able to rely on only one passage, or even use your general knowledge to avoid rereading at all.

> If researchers were to make a list of how positive emotions can lead to better health using the information provided in Passage A and Passage B, they would most likely include the fact that positive individuals:
>
> **A.** generally have stronger interpersonal relationships, increasing feelings of relaxation.
> **B.** possess higher levels of a hormone known to lower blood pressure and cholesterol.
> **C.** are less likely than negative individuals to experience second heart attacks.
> **D.** consistently demonstrate lower levels of inflammation in their arteries.

In order to answer this question, you must be able to identify a general point of agreement between the two passages, then take that understanding a step further to apply it to a new situation.

Starting by summing up the attitudes of both authors toward the relationship between emotions and health. You might say something like "correlation, NOT causation."

In other words, emotions are correlated with good/bad health, but they are not directly responsible for causing either disease or health. Rather, emotions influence behavior, and behavior influences health.

Passage A:

If you have a good sense of well-being, it's easier to maintain good habits: Exercising, eating a balanced diet and getting enough sleep, researchers say. (lines 32-35)

Passage B:

If a person is positive, he or she is more likely to show up for all the treatments, to have a better diet, to exercise. And if you're deeply depressed you sleep badly and that's bad for your health. (lines 75-79)

As a result, the correct answer to this question must be consistent with that indirect correlation. Only (A) fits that requirement. (B)-(D) all indicate more direct physical relationships, which are consistent with the idea of causation.

Practice Test 1

(answers p. 131)

Passage I

Prose Fiction: This passage is adapted from the novel *The Joy Luck Club* by Amy Tan (© 1989 by Amy Tan). The narrator is a girl named Waverly. Vincent is her brother.

On a cold spring afternoon, while walking home from school, I detoured through the playground at the end of our alley. I saw a group of old men, two seated across a folding table playing a game of chess, others smoking pipes, eating
5 peanuts, and watching. I ran home and grabbed Vincent's chess set, which was bound in a cardboard box with rubber bands. I also carefully selected two prized rolls of Life Savers. I came back to the park and approached a man who was observing the game.

10 "Want to play" I asked him. His face widened with surprise and he grinned as he looked at the box under my arm.

15 "Little sister, been a long time since I play with dolls," he said, smiling benevolently. I quickly put the box down next to him on the bench and displayed my retort.

Lau Po, as he allowed me to call him, turned out to be a
20 much better player than my brothers. I lost many games and many Life Savers. But over the weeks, with each diminishing roll of candies, I added new secrets. Lau Po gave me the names. The Double Attack from the East and West Shores. Throwing Stones on the Drowning Man. The
25 Sudden Meeting of the Clan. The Surprise from the Sleeping Guard. The Humble Servant Who Kills the King. Sand in the Eyes of Advancing Forces. A Double Killing Without Blood.

30 There were also the fine points of chess etiquette. Keep captured men in neat rows, as well-tended prisoners. Never announce "Check" with vanity, lest someone with an unseen sword slit your throat. Never hurl pieces into the sandbox after you have lost a game, because then you must
35 find them again, by yourself, after apologizing to all around you. By the end of the summer, Lau Po had taught me all he knew, and I had become a better chess player.

A small weekend crowd of Chinese people and tourists
40 would gather as I played and defeated my opponents one by one. My mother would join the crowds during these outdoor exhibition games. She sat proudly on the bench, telling my admirers with proper Chinese humility, "Is luck."

45 A man who watched me play in the park suggested that my mother allow me to play in local chess tournaments. My mother smiled graciously, an answer that meant nothing. I desperately wanted to go, but I bit back my tongue. I knew she would not let me play among strangers. So as we
50 walked home I said in a small voice that I didn't want to play in the local tournament. They would have American rules. If I lost, I would bring shame on my family.

"Is shame you fall down nobody push you," said my
55 mother.

During my first tournament, my mother sat with me in the front row as I waited for my turn. I frequently bounced my legs to unstick them from the cold metal seat of the
60 folding chair. When my name was called, I leapt up. My mother unwrapped something in her lap. It was her *chang*, a small tablet of red jade which held the sun's fire. "Is luck," she whispered, and tucked it into my dress pocket. I turned to my opponent, a fifteen year-old boy from Oakland. He
65 looked at me, wrinkling his nose.

As I began to play, the boy disappeared, the color ran out of the room, and I saw only my white pieces and his black ones waiting on the other side. A light wind began blowing
70 past my ears. It whispered secrets only I could hear.

"Blow from the South," it murmured. "The wind leaves no trail." I saw a clear path, the traps to avoid. The crowd rustled. "Shhh! Shhh!" said the corners of the room. The
75 wind blew stronger. "Throw sand from the East to distract him." The knight came forward ready for the sacrifice. The wind blew louder and louder. "Blow, blow, blow. He cannot see. He is blind now. Make him lean away from the wind so he can knock it down."

80 "Check," I said, as the wind roared with laughter. The wind died down to little puffs, my own breath.

* * *

85 My mother placed my first trophy next to a new plastic chess set that the neighborhood Tao society had given to me. As she wiped each piece with a soft cloth, she said, "Next time win more, lose less."

90 "Ma, it's not how many pieces you lose," I said. "Sometimes you need to lose pieces to get ahead."

"Better to lose less, see if you really need."

95 At the next tournament, I won again, but it was my mother who wore the triumphant grin.

"Lost eight pieces this time. Last time was eleven. What I tell you? Better off lose less!" I was annoyed, but I couldn't
100 say anything.

1. When Lau Po says "been a long time since I played with dolls" (line 15), he means that:

   A. he views chess primarily as a game for children.
   B. he is unaccustomed to playing chess against young girls like Waverly.
   C. he believes Waverly should pursue a more traditional pastime.
   D. he is no longer interested in playing chess.

2. The main purpose of the fourth paragraph (lines 19-28) is to:

   F. describe the disappointment that Waverly felt when she lost games to Lau Po.
   G. provide a list of the strategies that Waverly learned from Lau Po.
   H. explain how Waverly kept her chess games with Lau Po secret from her brothers.
   J. describe the reward system that Waverly and Lau Po established for their games.

3. In the last paragraph, Waverly most likely "couldn't say anything" because she:

   A. often found herself unable to speak in her mother's presence.
   B. was unable to refute her mother's argument logically.
   C. understood that her mother's knowledge of chess surpassed her own.
   D. believed that her mother was unlikely to pay attention if she spoke in English.

4. According to the passage, Waverly's first response to the suggestion that she compete in a chess tournament is to:

   F. smile graciously.
   G. plead to attend.
   H. remain silent.
   J. question her ability to compete.

5. As it is used in lines 67-68, the phrase *ran out of* most nearly means:

   A. dissolved.
   B. surrounded.
   C. competed against.
   D. vanished from.

6. The passage states that a player who has hurled chess pieces into the sandbox must:

   F. offer an apology, then pick up the pieces alone.
   G. be responsible for maintaining the other player's pieces in neat rows.
   H. never again utter "check" with vanity
   J. wear a *chang*.

7. Waverly suggests that her mother's "humility" (line 43) is:

   A. genuine because her mother wants to preserve Chinese traditions.
   B. genuine because her mother wants Waverly to appreciate her cultural heritage.
   C. false because Waverly states that her mother watched proudly as she defeated all her opponents.
   D. false because her mother did not want to be criticized for her daughter's arrogance.

8. In line 30, the phrase *fine points* is used to refer to:

   F. specific types of behavior that chess players are expected to exhibit.
   G. obscure regulations that no longer apply to modern chess games.
   H. a system of rules invented by Lau Po.
   J. subtle differences between Chinese and American forms of chess.

9. It is reasonable to infer that Waverly tells her mother she is afraid to "bring shame on her family" (line 52) because she:

   A. believes that expressing doubt in her abilities will cause her mother to relent.
   B. is becoming shy and uncertain in the United States.
   C. only wants to play chess against Lau Po.
   D. is concerned that she does not play chess well enough to compete against strangers.

10. Based on the passage as a whole, Waverly's mother could best be described as:

    F. warm and enthusiastic.
    G. simple and naïve.
    H. harsh and condescending.
    J. traditional yet opinionated.

113

Passage II

Social Science: Passage A is adapted from "Under Pressure: The Search for a Stress Vaccine," by Jonah Lehrer (© 2012 by *Wired*). Passage B is adapted from "What, Me Worry?" by Kristin Sainani (© 2014 by *Stanford Magazine*).

Chronic stress, it turns out, is an extremely dangerous

Passage A

condition. While stress doesn't cause any single disease — in fact, the causal link between stress and ulcers has been largely disproved—it makes most diseases significantly
5 worse. The list of ailments connected to stress is staggeringly diverse and includes everything from the common cold and lower-back pain to Alzheimer's disease, major depressive disorder, and heart attack. Stress hollows out our bones and atrophies our muscles. It triggers adult-
10 onset diabetes and may also be connected to high blood pressure. In fact, numerous studies of human longevity in developed countries have found that psychosocial factors such as stress are the single most important variable in determining the length of a life. It's not that genes and risk
15 factors like smoking don't matter. It's that our levels of stress matter more.

Furthermore, the effects of chronic stress directly counteract improvements in medical care and public
20 health. Antibiotics, for instance, are far less effective when our immune system is suppressed by stress; that heart surgery will work only if the patient can learn to shed stress. As pioneering stress researcher Robert Sapolsky notes, "You can give a guy a drug-coated stent, but if you
25 don't fix the stress problem, it won't really matter. For so many conditions, stress is the major long-term risk factor. Everything else is a short-term fix."

Passage B

According to a 2013 national survey by the American
30 Psychological Association, the average stress level among adults is 5.1 on a scale of 10; that's one and a half points above what the respondents judged to be healthy. Two-thirds of people say managing stress is important, and nearly that proportion had attempted to reduce their stress
35 in the previous five years. Yet only a little over a third say they succeeded at doing so. More discouraging, teens and young adults are experiencing higher levels of it, and also are struggling to manage it.

40 "Stress has a very bad reputation. It's in pretty bad shape, PR-wise," acknowledges Firdaus Dhabhar, an associate professor of psychiatry and behavioral science at Stanford. "And justifiably so," he adds.

45 Much of what we know about the physical and mental toll of chronic stress stems from seminal work by Robert Sapolsky beginning in the late 1970s. Sapolsky, a neuroendocrinologist, was among the first to make the connection that the hormones released during the fight-or-
50 flight response—the ones that helped our ancestors avoid becoming dinner—have deleterious effects when the stress is severe and sustained. Especially insidious, chronic exposure to one of these hormones, cortisol, causes brain changes that make it increasingly difficult to shut the stress
55 response down.

But take heart: Recent research paints a different portrait of stress, one in which it indeed has a positive side. "There's good stress, there's tolerable stress, and there's toxic stress,"
60 says Bruce McEwen of Rockefeller University, an expert on stress and the brain who trained both Sapolsky and Dhabhar. Situations we typically perceive as stressful—a confrontation with a co-worker, the pressure to perform, a to-do list that's too long—are not the toxic type of stress
65 that's been linked to serious health issues such as cardiovascular disease, autoimmune disorders, severe depression and cognitive impairment. Short bouts of this sort of everyday stress can actually be a good thing: Just think of the exhilaration of the deadline met or the
70 presentation crushed, the triumph of holding it all together. And, perhaps not surprisingly, it turns out that beating yourself up about being stressed is counterproductive, as worrying about the negative consequences can in itself exacerbate any ill effects.

11. Which of the following statements about human longevity in developed countries is best supported by Passage A?

    A. It is consistently higher than in developing countries.
    B. It is unaffected by individual behaviors.
    C. It is less influenced by genetics than it is by psychosocial factors.
    D. It is directly correlated with adult-onset diabetes.

12. According to Passage A, a major effect of stress is to:

    F. cause muscles to weaken.
    G. increase sensitivity to antibiotics.
    H. create small changes in a person's genome.
    J. make some patients ineligible for surgery.

13. The main function of the quotation in lines 24-27 of Passage A is to:

    A. point out that certain types of surgery are often ineffective in the short term.
    B. indicate the disproportionate impact of stress on the body's ability to recover from illness.
    C. present a compelling argument for delaying surgery in severely ill patients.
    D. suggest that the benefits of drug-coated stents have been largely overestimated.

14. As it appears in line 58 of Passage B, the phrase "take heart" most nearly refers to the fact that:

    F. people who suffer from heart disease should take care to avoid stressful situations.
    G. people should feel reassured to discover that stress can have beneficial effects.
    H. small amounts of toxic stress can lead to a sense of exhilaration.
    J. the differences between types of stress are less significant than they were once thought to be.

15. The main purpose of the first paragraph of Passage B (lines 29-38) is to:

    A. describe an impending public health crisis.
    B. call attention to the effects of chronic stress on teens and young adults.
    C. suggest that it is impossible to remove stress entirely from daily life.
    D. emphasize the pervasiveness of stress across a range of groups.

16. Based on the information in Passage B, it is reasonable to infer that prior to Robert Sapolsky's research in the 1970s, researchers:

    A. were unaware that changes to the brain caused by cortisol can have harmful and long-lasting effects.
    B. did not recognize that stress hormones allowed human ancestors to avoid attacks from predators.
    C. questioned the relationship between toxic stress and the development of disease.
    D. had not yet identified the connection between cortisol and the fight-or-flight response.

17. Which of the following terms in Passage B is used more figuratively than literally?

    F. "scale" (line 31)
    G. "struggling" (line 38)
    H. "released" (line 49)
    J. "paints" (line 57)

18. A similarity between the passages is that they both:

    F. call attention to significant periods in the history of science.
    G. describe key changes that stress causes in the brain.
    H. discuss research conducted by a key figure in the field of stress research.
    J. emphasize the role of cortisol in the body's response to stress.

19. An element of Passage B that is not present in Passage A is a reference to what aspect of stress?

    A. Impact on public health
    B. Potential benefits
    C. Physical effects
    D. Interaction with medication

20. If health advisors were recruited to help recipients of the stents described in Passage A recover from surgery using recent findings described in Passage B, those counselors would most likely recommend that the patients:

    F. take supplements to suppress cortisol production.
    G. gradually expose themselves to stressful situations.
    H. avoid dwelling on their anxieties.
    J. regularly monitor their stress on a 10-point scale.

Passage III

Humanities: This passage is adapted from an article titled "Ralph Waldo Emerson: Beyond the Greeting Cards" by Danny Heitman (© 2013 by Danny Heitman).

As a teenager in 1960, Clyde Edgerton was trying to find a name for the doubts he was feeling about his conventional, small-town life in Bethesda, North Carolina. Then, a high school assignment offered up a tutor for life. Edgerton's
5 epiphany came while reading Ralph Waldo Emerson's "Nature."

In Emerson, Edgerton found someone who let him know that questioning orthodox belief was not only
10 acceptable, but vital. "My mind was set afire as if soaked in gasoline," Edgerton would recall many years later in an essay. "Emerson had served me up a bowl of intellectual rebellion at just the right time in my young life." The encounter steered Edgerton toward college, which he had
15 planned to skip, and onward to a successful career as the novelist behind such celebrated works as *Raney* and *Walking Across Egypt*.

"Here was a writer who wrote about ideas—ideas that
20 heated my blood," Edgerton writes of Emerson. "He was moral, but not dictatorial and narrow. He was kind. He loved the world, and it seemed as if he had written some sentences for no one but me."

25 Edgerton's testimonial seems all the more vivid because of its rarity. Few people these days talk deeply about Emerson, the quintessential nineteenth-century New Englander, as an agent of passion or personal revolution. Emerson, a founding father of American letters, who
30 famously declared that "every hero becomes a bore at last," would perhaps not be too surprised to learn that even some of his modern-day admirers occasionally find him boring, too.

35 In "The American Scholar," an address he gave at Harvard in 1837, however, Emerson captivated his listeners when he urged them to do their own thinking instead of using imported ideas from the Old World. Emerson's point was not that English and European thinking was uniformly
40 bad; he had, after all, derived many of his own insights from the German intellectuals Johann Goethe and Immanuel Kant, and he was also an avid student of Eastern religion. But Emerson argued that all ideas should be tested by individual experience, and not merely accepted based on the
45 power of precedent.

If Emerson's life, despite its periods of public controversy and private pain, seemed placid when compared with the lives of many other writers, it is perhaps because
50 his home thrived on order and unassuming routine, making its drama less visible. Phillip Lopate, a modern-day essayist who counts himself a big Emerson fan, suggests that "Emerson has become an afterthought in the American literary canon because he lacks that outsider romance of our
55 other mid-nineteenth century giants. We tend to value renegades like Thoreau, recluses like Dickinson, misunderstood visionaries like Melville, expansive bards like Whitman."

60 Emerson's stability made him a natural mentor to writers such as Thoreau—who borrowed Emerson's land to make his famous home near Walden Pond—and fellow transcendentalist Bronson Alcott. Emerson, wrote biographer Robert D. Richardson Jr., would always
65 remember Thoreau as his best friend, "even when his memory loss was so far advanced that he could not pull up the name." Later published in essay form, Emerson's tribute to the author of *Walden* exhibits a directness and vulnerability seldom found in Emerson's other published
70 writings.

The Library of America published a two-volume selection of Emerson's journals in 2010, prompting Lopate to take a fresh look at a writer who had previously left him
75 cold. "Truthfully, I never felt that close to Emerson in the past," Lopate confessed. "I admired his prose style, but his essays seemed too impersonal for my taste. They sounded oracular, abstract, dizzyingly inspired, like visionary sermons: the thinking and language spectacular, the man
80 somehow missing. It took reading his journals to appreciate the man and the work."

Like Lopate, contemporary nature essayist Scott Russell Sanders thinks that Emerson's most appealing presence rests
85 not in his essays, but in his journals. "When I first read a handful of his essays in college, I didn't much care for Ralph Waldo Emerson," Sanders writes. "He seemed too high-flown, too cocksure, too earnest. I couldn't imagine he had ever sweated or doubted. His sentences rang with a
90 magisterial certainty that I could never muster."

Even so, Emerson probably wouldn't protest too much Lopate's assessment of his legacy: "He wrote some of the
95 best reflective prose we have; he was a hero of intellectual labor, a loyal friend and, taking all flaws into account, a good egg."

21. All of the following are mentioned in the passage as influences on Emerson EXCEPT

    A. Johann Goethe.
    B. Immanuel Kant.
    C. "The American Scholar."
    D. Eastern religion.

22. Based on the information provided in lines 47-51, it is reasonable to infer that compared to Emerson's home life, the home lives of many other writers were more:

    F. conventional.
    G. exciting.
    H. mysterious.
    J. praiseworthy.

23. The passage indicates that prior to 2010, Phillip Lopate viewed Emerson's writing as:

    A. detached and inaccessible.
    B. guarded and secretive.
    C. intriguing yet alarming.
    D. passionate and heartwarming.

24. The passage suggests that members of the American literary canon are typically valued for their:

    F. outsider status.
    G. reflective nature.
    H. stylistic brilliance.
    J. social conformity.

25. When Edgerton says that his "mind was set afire as if soaked in gasoline" (lines 10-11), he most nearly means that he:

    A. was disturbed by Emerson's tendency to question orthodox beliefs.
    B. found the meaning of Emerson's writing difficult to understand.
    C. felt thrilled and inspired by Emerson's ideas.
    D. was unable to concentrate on the most vital parts of Emerson's work.

26. According to the passage, Scott Russell Sanders believes that Emerson's most appealing writing is found in his:

    F. essays.
    G. journals.
    H. tribute to the author of *Walden*.
    J. address given at Harvard in 1837.

27. The passage indicates Emerson believed English and European thinking:

    A. should be combined with insights from personal experience.
    B. could not be applied to everyday life in the United States.
    C. relied excessively on the ideas of Johann Goethe and Immanuel Kant.
    D. was outdated and worthless.

28. The main function of the sixth paragraph (lines 47-58) in relation to the passage as a whole is to:

    F. describe how Emerson's private life differed from his public life.
    G. compare Emerson's literary style to the style of his contemporaries.
    H. account for Emerson's relative lack of popularity among American writers.
    J. explain how Emerson acquired the reputation of a romantic outsider.

29. As it is used in 39, the word *uniformly* most nearly means

    A. independently.
    B. methodically.
    C. fairly.
    D. invariably.

30. Statements by Phillip Lopate and Scott Russell Sanders suggest that Emerson's essays differed from his journals in that his essays were:

    F. lofty and exalted.
    G. soothing and engaging.
    H. tentative and doubtful.
    J. personal and reflective.

Passage IV

Natural Science: This passage is adapted from an article titled "What Bees Tell Us About Global Climate Change" by Sharon Tregaskis (© 2010 by *Johns Hopkins Magazine*).

Standing in the apiary on the grounds of the U.S. Department of Agriculture's Bee Research Laboratory in Beltsville, Maryland, Wayne Esaias digs through the canvas shoulder bag leaning against his leg in search of the cable
[5] he uses to download data. It's dusk as he runs the cord from his laptop—precariously perched on the beam of a cast-iron platform scale—to a small, battery-operated data logger attached to the spring inside the scale's steel column. In the 1800s, a scale like this would have weighed sacks of grain
[10] or crates of apples, peaches, and melons. Since arriving at the USDA's bee lab in January 2007, this scale has been loaded with a single item: a colony of *Apis mellifera*, the fuzzy, black-and-yellow honey bee. An attached, 12-bit recorder captures the hive's weight to within a 10th of a
[15] pound, along with a daily register of relative ambient humidity and temperature.

On this late January afternoon, during a comparatively balmy respite between the blizzards that dumped several
[20] feet of snow on the Middle Atlantic states, the bees, their honey, and the wooden boxes in which they live weigh 94.5 pounds. In mid-July, as last year's unusually long nectar flow finally ebbed, the whole contraption topped out at 275 pounds, including nearly 150 pounds of honey. "Right now,
[25] the colony is in a cluster about the size of a soccer ball," says Esaias, who's kept bees for nearly two decades and knows without lifting the lid what's going on inside this hive. "The center of the cluster is where the queen is, and they're keeping her at 93 degrees—the rest are just hanging
[30] there, tensing their flight muscles to generate heat." Provided that they have enough calories to fuel their winter workout, a healthy colony can survive as far north as Anchorage, Alaska. "They slowly eat their way up through the winter," he says. "It's a race: Will they eat all their
[35] honey before the nectar flows, or not?"

To make sure their charges win that race, apiarists have long relied on scale hives for vital management clues. By tracking daily weight variations, a beekeeper can discern
[40] when the colony needs a nutritional boost to carry it through lean times, whether to add extra combs for honey storage, and even detect incursions by marauding robber bees—all without disturbing the colony. A graph of the hive
weight—which can increase by as much as 35 pounds a da
[45] in some parts of the United States during peak nect flow—reveals the date on which the bees' foraging w most productive and provides a direct record of successf pollination. "Around here, the bees make their living in t month of May," says Esaias, noting that his bees ofte
[50] achieve daily spikes of 25 pounds, the maximum Maryland. "There's almost no nectar coming in for the re of the year."

A scientist by training and career oceanographer
NASA, Esaias established the Mink Hollow Apiary in h
[55] Highland, Maryland, backyard in 1992 with a trio of han me-down hives and an antique platform scale much like t one at the Beltsville bee lab. Ever since, he's maintained meticulous record of the bees' daily weight, as well weather patterns and such details as his efforts to keep the
[60] healthy. In late 2006, honey bees nationwide beg disappearing in an ongoing syndrome dubbed colo collapse disorder (CCD). Entire hives went empty as be inexplicably abandoned their young and their hone Commercial beekeepers reported losses up to 90 perce
[65] and the large-scale farmers who rely on honey bees ensure rich harvests of almonds, apples, and sunflowe became very, very nervous. Looking for clues, Esai turned to his own records. While the resulting graphs thre no light on the cause of CCD, a staggering trend emerge
[70] In the span of just 15 seasons, the date on which his Mi Hollow bees brought home the most nectar had shifted two weeks—from late May to the middle of the month. was shocked when I plotted this up," he says. "It was rig
[75] under my nose, going on the whole time."

The epiphany would lead Esaias to launch a series research collaborations, featuring honey bees and oth pollinators, to investigate the relationships among plan
[80] pollinators, and weather patterns. Already, the work h begun to reveal insights into the often unintend consequences of human interventions in natural a agricultural ecosystems, and exposed significant gaps how we understand the effect climate change will have
[85] everything from food production to terrestrial ecology.

31. According to the passage, honey bees generate heat by:

    A. huddling together in the hive.
    B. eating nectar.
    C. tensing muscles used for flight.
    D. vibrating their stomachs.

32. The passage indicates that Esaias's first hives at the Mink Hollow Apiary were most likely:

    F. about the size of a soccer ball.
    G. acquired from another bee-keeper.
    H. most productive in mid May.
    J. unusually nervous.

33. Which of the following questions is NOT answered in the passage?

    A. In what year was colony collapse disorder (CCD) first observed?
    B. What is an alternate name for the honey bee?
    C. Why did Wayne Esaias decide to study honey bees?
    D. Can honey bee colonies survive in cold climates?

34. In line 50, the word *spikes* most nearly means:

    F. increases.
    G. stings.
    H. developments.
    J. exaggerations.

35. The passage indicates that in order to track his hives' weight, Esaias uses:

    A. instruments developed specifically for bee-keepers.
    B. a combination of old and new technologies.
    C. sacks of grain and fruit crates.
    D. a digital scale.

36. The epiphany mentioned in line 77 most directly refers to the fact that:

    F. Esaias's graphs were able to shed light on the the origins of CCD.
    G. changing weather patterns can have. devastating effects on the natural world.
    H. there are significant gaps in the existing explanations of climate change.
    J. the date on which Esaias's bees collected the greatest amount of nectar was two weeks earlier than expected.

37. The passage indicates that by using scale hives, apiarists can determine all of the following EXCEPT:

    A. nutritional deficiencies.
    B. the time when robber bees will attack.
    C. the need for additional storage combs.
    D. peak foraging productivity.

38. Which of the following statements best describes how the fourth paragraph (lines 54-75) functions in context of the passage as a whole:

    F. It shifts the focus of the passage to a discussion of a problem afflicting the honey bee population.
    G. It explains how Esaias was inspired to start the Mink Hollow Apiary.
    H. It describes the process by which honeybees pollinate plants and fruit trees.
    J. It refutes a popular explanation for the causes of CCD.

39. It can be reasonably inferred that between January and July, the weight of a box containing a bee hive can vary by approximately:

    A. 95 lbs.
    B. 150 lbs.
    C. 180 lbs.
    D. 275 lbs.

40. Information in the passage suggests that in 1992, bees collected the largest amount of nectar in:

    F. mid May.
    G. late January.
    H. mid July.
    J. late May.

Practice Test 2

(answers p. 137)

Passage I

Prose Fiction: This passage is adapted from the novel *"The Painted Drum* by Louise Erdrich (© 2005 by Louise Erdrich). The narrator is a woman named Faye; Elsie is her mother.

I'm home before eleven, like a good teen on a demure date. The light is on in the first-floor living room where Elsie likes to sit and listen to music. She has Satie on. The master of punctuation. When I walk into the room she
5   stiffens in her chair, casts her gaze upon me, and says, in that parental voice even grown children dread to hear, "Sit down, we have something to talk about."

"Can it wait?" It must be that she has seen the drum, and although I know it is inevitable, I really don't want to talk
10 about it tonight.

Elsie stares at me, trying not to blink. The music has become the backdrop to a suspense movie. All jagged exclamation points. I turn it off and sit down across from
15 her. She is wearing an old pink chenille bathrobe and elegant turquoise earrings.

"You left these in." I tap my earlobes.

20 "On purpose," she says.

"Oh?"

25 She pauses in an ominous way before she speaks. "Years ago, I nearly stole these earrings from a client."

I turn away and busy myself examining the folds and stitches of one of her more complex afghans. She
30 continues.

"I was very tempted. I happened to have recognized the earrings from a little-known Curtis photograph. It wasn't that the earrings are so valuable, but that they'd lain close
35 the girl's neck, the subject, and if I had them it seemed, I felt, as though I was part of his work too."

"I took the drum for similar reasons."

40 "Oh, no doubt." Her voice is dry. After an empty pause, she prompts, "When are you planning to return it?"

"I'm not."

45 She throws her hands up, lets them fall to her knees and hang down, limp rags of dismay.

"It would look odd if I just brought I back now. No one knows it's missing."

50 "Nonsense." You could say you had it repaired."

"Well, I could. You're right."

55 "But you won't. You don't want to."

"No."

"What are you going to do with it?" she asks, and I
60 respond before I've thought out my answer. The resolute note in my voice surprises me.

"For now, keep it. Later we'll find the rightful owner."

65 She shrugs and seems to think aloud. "Well, yes...it's Ojibwe and the fact that Tatro spent his life as an Indian agent on our home reservation probably makes your guess as to its origin, maybe even your intention, fairly reasonable." She opens her arms as though surrendering.
70 "Good luck to you, then. Not only do I want no part of it, I'm thinking of bringing it back to the Tatro's myself. You could purchase it, you know. I bought the earrings."

"Before or after you told the family that they were in a
75 famous photograph?"

I think I've got her, but she refuses to be embarrassed.

"Only a fool would have revealed that. Of course I got
80 them for a good price."

It's no use, and I hate being at odds with her. Still the idea that she would actually take it upon herself to return the drum makes me regress a little. "Don't you touch that
85 drum!"

"You exasperate me." She closes her mouth in that tight, straight line that means we're finished arguing. This is as angry as we ever get, and we both know it won't last.
90

Sure enough, over breakfast, Elsie tells me that she's decided, upon reflection, that the fact that the drum was stolen from our own people is a piece of synchronicity so disturbing that she now understands how I was motivated.
95 I, on the other hand, am moved to tell her that I am sorry to have possibly compromised her also in the theft, as it is both of our business reputations at stake, and even (now that I know she won't hold me to it) that I'll consider returning the drum. But she says that she wouldn't think of
100 returning it, that she's always wondered exactly how it was that Jewett Parker Tatro acquired his hoard, and that maybe in discovering more about this particular drum we will find that out. She's willing to help me, in fact, learn its origins.
105

Elsie has ideas. She is spilling over with ideas and with lists of people and with plans to see them. "I'm thinking of old Shaawano, gone now" she says, "and Mrs. String. Her first name is Chook and she's related to the old man and
110 married to Mike String. Lots of the people have passed on, of course, the ones who would know. But to lose or be swindled out a drum like this is no small thing.

1. The passage suggests that narrator took the drum because she:

   A. believed she could sell it for a high price.
   B. intended to have it repaired.
   C. felt a personal connection to it.
   D. was determined to find its rightful owner.

2. Who does the passage indicate owned the drum before the narrator acquired it?

   F. Elsie
   G. old Shaawano
   H. Mrs. String
   J. Jewett Parker Tatro

3. As it is used in line 96, the word *compromised* most nearly means:

   A. condemned.
   B. put at risk.
   C. inquired about.
   D. came to an agreement.

4. In context of the passage, Elsie's statement that she got the earrings for a good price implies that she:

   F. did not reveal that they had appeared in the Curtis photograph.
   G. wanted to avoid remaining at odds with the narrator.
   H. was unaware of their monetary value.
   J. was embarrassed that she had nearly stolen them.

5. The passage indicates that arguments between the narrator and Elsie are usually:

   A. violent and unpredictable.
   B. a source of frequent exasperation.
   C. mild and short-lived.
   D. fundamentally irresolvable.

6. The passage most directly suggests that the narrator will "consider returning the drum" (lines 98-99) because she:

   F. does not want her business reputation to be damaged.
   G. wishes to protect Elsie from the potential consequences of the theft.
   H. wishes to encourage Elsie's curiosity about the drum's origins.
   J. knows that she will not be required to keep her word.

7. The passages most directly suggests that Satie is:

   A. a composer whose music Elsie enjoys listening to.
   B. the artist who created the earrings Elsie is wearing.
   C. a writer whose works have influenced the narrator's life.
   D. a photographer renowned for producing images of the Ojibwe.

8. Which of the following statements best describes the function of the second to last paragraph (lines 91-104) in context of the passage as a whole?

   F. It offers a comparison between the narrator's relationship with Elsie and her relationship with the Tatro family.
   G. It provides support for an idea introduced at the end of the previous paragraph.
   H. It outlines the steps taken by the narrator and Elsie during their search for the drum's origins.
   J. It describes how the narrator came to suspect that the drum had been stolen from the Ojibwe people.

9. Based on the information on the passage as a whole, it is most reasonable to infer that Elsie left her earrings in on purpose because she:

   A. wanted to call attention to the fact that they had been bought rather than stolen.
   B. was unable to remove them with her withered hands.
   C. intended to dissuade the narrator from giving the drum to the Tatro family.
   D. wanted to remind the narrator that they had appeared in the Curtis photograph.

10. Which of the following best describes the shift in Elsie's attitude, as it occurs over the course of the passage?

    F. Irritation to indifference
    G. Dismay to enthusiasm
    H. Curiosity to disbelief
    J. Skepticism to reverence

Passage II

Social Science: This passage is adapted from the book *Thinking in Pictures* by Temple Grandin (© 2006 by Temple Grandin).

The idea that people have different thinking patterns is not new. Francis Galton, in *Inquiries into Human Faculty and Development*, wrote that while some people see vivid mental pictures, for others "the idea is not felt to be mental pictures, but rather symbols of facts. In people with low pictorial imagery, they would remember their breakfast table but they could not see it."

It wasn't until I went to college that I realized some people are completely verbal and think only in words. I first suspected this when I read an article in a science magazine about the development of tools in prehistoric humans. Some renowned scientist speculated that humans had to develop language before they could develop tools. I thought this was ridiculous, and this article gave me the first inkling that my thought processes were truly different from those of many other people. When I invent things, I do not use language. Some other people think in vividly detailed pictures, but most think in a combination of words and vague, generalized pictures.

For example, many people see a generalized generic church rather than specific churches and steeples when they hear or read the word *steeple*. Their thought patterns move from a general concept to specific examples. I used to become very frustrated when a verbal thinker could not understand something I was trying to express because he or she couldn't see the picture that was crystal clear to me. Further, my mind constantly revises general concepts as I add new information to my memory library. It's like getting a new version of software for the computer. My mind readily accepts the new "software," though I have observed that some people often do not readily accept new information.

Unlike those of most people, my thoughts move from video-like, specific images to generalizations and concepts. For example, my concept of dogs is inextricably linked to every dog I've ever known. It's as if I have a card catalogue of dogs I have seen, complete with pictures, which continually grows as I add more examples to my video library. If I think about Great Danes, the first memory that pops into my head is Dansk, the Great Dane owned by the headmaster at my high school. The next Great Dane I visualize is Helga, who was Dansk's replacement. The next is my aunt's dog in Arizona, and my final image comes from an advertisement for Fitwell seat covers that features that kind of dog. My memories usually appear in my imagination in strict chronological order, and the images I visualize are always specific. There is no generic generalized Great Dane.

However, not all people with autism are highly visual thinkers, nor do they all process information this way. People throughout the world are on a continuum of visualization skills ranging from next to none, to seeing vague generalized pictures, to seeing semi-specific pictures, to seeing, as in my case, in very specific pictures.

I'm always forming new visual images when I invent new equipment or think of something novel and amusing. I can take images that I have seen, rearrange them, and create new pictures. For example, I can imagine what a dip vat would look like modeled on computer graphics by placing it on my memory of a friend's computer screen. Since his computer is not programmed to do the fancy 3-D rotary graphics, I take computer graphics I have seen on TV or in the movies and superimpose them in my memory. In my visual imagination the dip vat will appear in the kind of high-quality computer graphics shown on *Star Trek*. I can redraw it on the computer screen in my mind. I can even duplicate the cartoonlike, three-dimensional skeletal image on the computer screen or imagine the dip vat as a videotape of the real thing.

Similarly, I learned how to draw engineering designs by closely observing a very talented draftsman when we worked together at the same feed yard construction company. David was able to render the most fabulous drawings effortlessly. After I left the company, I was forced to do all my own drafting. By studying David's drawings for many hours and photographing them in my memory, I was able to emulate David's drawing style. I laid some of his drawings out so I could look at them while I drew my first design. Then I drew my new plan and copied his style. After making three or four drawings, I no longer had to have his drawings out on the table. My video memory was now fully programmed.

11. Based on the information in the passage, which of the following statements best describes how the author thinks?

    A. She begins with broad concepts, then refers to specific images.
    B. She primarily uses images but sometimes uses words to help her recall specific events.
    C. She thinks in a combination of words and vague, generalized images.
    D. She relies on a series of vivid images from which she eventually creates general concepts.

12. The author indicates that in comparison to David's drawings, her own drawings:

    F. required much more effort.
    G. were made entirely from memories.
    H. primarily featured animals.
    J. included superimposed images.

13. Which of the following is NOT mentioned in the passage as an influence on the narrator's concept of Great Danes?

    A. Helga.
    B. her aunt's dog.
    C. computer graphics.
    D. a media image.

14. The author's reaction to the work of "some renowned scientist" (line 13) can best be described as one of:

    F. scorn.
    G. enthusiasm.
    H. awe.
    J. resignation.

15. Based on the passage, it is reasonable to infer that the author's idea of a steeple would be based on:

    A. a generalized concept of a steeple.
    B. an amalgam of all the steeples she had ever seen.
    C. a combination of words and general pictures.
    D. computer software.

16. The author suggests that among people with autism, the tendency to think exclusively in images:

    F. is an extremely unusual trait.
    G. has become more pronounced since the invention of television.
    H. is considerably more common than it is in people without autism.
    J. occurs as frequently as it does in the general population.

17. As it is used in line 87, the word *emulate* most nearly means:

    A. mimic.
    B. praise.
    C. include.
    D. comprehend.

18. The primary function of the second paragraph (lines 9-21) in context of the passage as a whole is to:

    F. discuss the author's disillusionment with mainstream scientific research.
    G. explain how the author learned to invent things using detailed pictures.
    H. describe how the author discovered that her thought processes were very different from those of most other people.
    J. compare and contrast the author's work with that of a renowned scientist.

19. The quotation by Francis Galton suggests that people with low pictorial imagery:

    A. have a limited perception of color.
    B. do not see vivid mental pictures.
    C. recall images rather than facts.
    D. can only visualize generic images.

20. The author states that events in her memories occur:

    A. less vividly than the actual events.
    B. at a distance, as if she were watching a computer screen.
    C. in a random and disjoined manner.
    D. in chronological order.

Passage III

Humanities: Passage A is adapted from "Why Fiction is Good for You" by Jonathan Gottschall (© 2012 *The Boston Globe*. Passage B is adapted from "The Business Case for Reading Novels" by Anne Kreamer (© 2012 by *Harvard Business Review*).

Passage A

Is fiction good for us? We spend huge chunks of our lives immersed in novels, films, TV shows, and other forms of fiction. Some see this as a positive thing, arguing that made-up stories cultivate our mental and moral

5 development. But others have argued that fiction is mentally and ethically corrosive. It's an ancient question: Does fiction build the morality of individuals and societies, or does it break it down?

10 This controversy has been flaring up — sometimes literally, in the form of book burnings — ever since Plato tried to ban fiction from his ideal republic. In 1961, Newton Minow famously said that television was not working in "the public interest" because its "formula

15 comedies about totally unbelievable families, blood and thunder, mayhem, western bad men, western good men, private eyes, gangsters, and cartoons" amounted to a "vast wasteland." And what he said of TV programming has also been said, over the centuries, of novels, theater, comic

20 books, and films: They are not in the public interest.

Until recently, we've only been able to guess about the actual psychological effects of fiction on individuals and society. But new research in psychology and broad-based literary analysis is finally taking questions about morality

25 out of the realm of speculation.

This research consistently shows that fiction does mold us. The more deeply we are cast under a story's spell, the

30 more potent its influence. In fact, fiction seems to be more effective at changing beliefs than nonfiction, which is designed to persuade through argument and evidence. Studies show that when we read nonfiction, we read with our shields up. We are critical and skeptical. But when we

35 are absorbed in a story, we drop our intellectual guard. We are moved emotionally, and this seems to make us rubbery and easy to shape.

But perhaps the most impressive finding is just how

40 fiction shapes us. Fiction enhances our ability to understand other people; it promotes a deep morality. More peculiarly, fiction's happy endings seem to warp our sense of reality. They make us believe in a lie: that the world is more just than it actually is. But believing that lie has

45 important effects for society — and it may even help explain why humans tell stories in the first place.

Passage B

I've been a devoted, even fanatical reader of fiction my whole life, but sometimes I feel like I'm wasting time if spend an evening immersed in Lee Child's newest thriller

50 or re-reading *The Great Gatsby*. Shouldn't I be plowing through my in-box? Or getting the hang of some new productivity app? Or catching up on my back issues of *The Economist*? That slight feeling of self-indulgence tha haunts me when I'm reading fake stories about fake peopl

55 is what made me so grateful to stumble on a piece i *Scientific American Mind* by cognitive psychologist Keith Oatley extolling the practical benefits to be derive particularly from consuming fiction.

60 Over the past decade, academic researchers have gathered data indicating that fiction-reading activate neuronal pathways in the brain that measurably help th reader better understand real human emotion — improvin his or her overall social skillfulness. It turns out that whe

65 Henry James, more than a century ago, defended the valu of fiction by saying that "a novel is a direct impression c life," he was more right than he knew.

Theory of mind, the ability to interpret and respond t

70 those different from us is plainly critical to success particularly in a globalized economy. The imperative to tr to understand others' points of view — to be empathetic – is essential in any collaborative enterprise. Emotions als have an impact on the bottom line. A 1996 study publishe

75 in the journal *Training and Development* assessing th value of training workers at a manufacturing plant i emotional management skills — teaching employees t focus on how their work affects others rather than simpl on getting the job done — found that union grievanc

80 filings were reduced by two-thirds while productivit increased substantially.

And if you want your diet of fiction to be specificall relevant to work, there is a body of great literature abou

85 business and organizational behavior. For instanc Anthony Trollope's *The Way We Live Now*, inspired b 19th century financial scandals among the British elit resonates powerfully today. In his autobiography, Trollop wrote that "a certain class of dishonesty, dishonest

90 magnificent in its proportions, and climbing into hig places, has become at the same time so rampant and s splendid that there seems to be reason for fearing that me and women will be taught to feel that dishonesty, if it ca

become splendid, will cease to be abominable. If
dishonesty can live in a gorgeous palace with pictures on
all its walls, and gems in all its cupboards, with marble and
ivory in all its corners, and can give Apician dinners, and
get into Parliament, and deal in millions, then dishonesty is
not disgraceful, and the man dishonest after such a fashion
is not a low scoundrel. Instigated, I say, by some such
reflections as these, I sat down in my new house to write
"The Way We Live Now." Seems fairly *au courant** to me.

*A French expression meaning "current."

| Questions 21-24 ask about Passage A. | Questions 25-27 ask about Passage B. |

21. The main purpose of the first paragraph of Passage A
is to:

 A. explain how fiction promotes intellectual and
 moral development.
 B. criticize the role of the media in contemporary
 society.
 C. present a longstanding debate about the merits
 of fiction.
 D. trace the development of fiction since ancient
 times.

22. As it is used in lines 33-34, the phrase *with our
shields up* most nearly refers to:

 F. the sense of morality that allows us to understand
 other people's emotions.
 G. authors' ability to rely on their own preferences
 rather than the opinions of critics.
 H. the psychological barrier that prevents readers
 from being persuaded by arguments based on
 logic and evidence.
 J. the sense of emotional connection that makes
 readers of fiction easy to shape.

23. According to Passage A, fiction was traditionally
considered:

 A. crucial to the public interest.
 B. lacking in social value.
 C. excessively formulaic.
 D. more compelling than non-fiction.

24. Passage A indicates that one characteristic of
fictional works is that they:

 F. reflect social and political controversies.
 G. make readers critical and skeptical.
 H. present a distorted vision of the world.
 J. cause readers to trust new acquaintances more
 quickly.

25. The author of Passage B states that fiction improves
social skillfulness by:

 A. altering pathways in the brain.
 B. reducing feelings of self-indulgence.
 C. imparting particular codes of conduct.
 D. helping readers to acquire more refined tastes.

26. Which of the following statements best expresses the
opinion the author of Passage B seems to have about
Henry James and Anthony Trollope:

 F. They were responsible for changing public
 opinions about fiction.
 G. Their works were popular among readers of their
 own time but are no longer relevant today.
 H. They blurred traditional lines between art and
 business.
 J. They expressed enduring truths about life and
 society.

27. In context of the passage as a whole, which of the
following statements best describes the shift that
occurs in the second paragraph of Passage B (lines
60-67)?

 A. It moves from a description of a personal
 experience to an objective, third-person narration.
 B. It moves from a description of Keith Oatley's
 findings to an analysis of those findings.
 C. It moves from a focus on the importance of
 science to a focus on the importance of literature.
 D. It moves from a discussion of contemporary
 works to a consideration of classic works.

28. It is reasonable to infer that the author of Passage A and the author of Passage B would agree that fiction:

F. encourages an idealized view of human relations.
G. facilitates the ability to see the world from alternate perspectives.
H. accurately depicts a wide variety of real-life situations.
J. promotes unreasonable expectations about fairness and justice.

29. In comparison to the tone of Passage B, the tone of Passage A is more:

A. carefree.
B. empathetic.
C. scornful.
D. objective.

30. Another writer made the following statement about endings:

> Happiness is a sleight of hand designed to make you believe in fairy tales. But there's no happily ever after.

The author of which passage would be most likely to agree with this quotation?

F. The author of passage A, because it emphasizes the relationship between fiction and morality.
G. The author of Passage A, because it points out that real life is less fair than fiction implies.
H. The author of Passage B, because it suggests that reading fiction is self-indulgent.
J. The author of Passage B, because it indicates that reading fiction can help people manage their emotions.

Passage IV

Natural Science: This passage is adapted from an article titled "Solving the Mystery of Death Valley's Walking Rocks" by Michael Anft (© 2011 by *Johns Hopkins Magazine*).

For six decades, observers have been confounded by the movement of large rocks across a dry lake bed in California's Death Valley National Park. Leaving flat trails behind them, rocks that weigh up to 100 pounds
5 seemingly do Michael Jackson's moonwalk across the valley's sere, cracked surface, sometimes traveling more than 100 yards. Without a body of water to pick them up and move them, the rocks at Racetrack Playa, a flat space between the valley's high cliffs, have been the subject of
10 much speculation, including whether they have been relocated by human pranksters or space aliens. The rocks have become the desert equivalent of Midwestern crop circles.

15 "They really are a curiosity," says Ralph Lorenz, a planetary scientist at the Applied Physics Laboratory. "Some [people] have mentioned UFOs. But I've always believed that this is something science could solve."

20 It has tried. One theory holds that the rocks are blown along by powerful winds. Another posits that the wind pushes thin sheets of ice, created when the desert's temperatures dip low enough to freeze water from a rare rainstorm, and the rocks go along for the ride. But neither
25 theory is rock solid. Winds at the playa aren't strong enough—some scientists believe that they'd have to be 100 miles per hour or more—to blow the rocks across the valley. And rocks subject to the "ice sailing theory" wouldn't create trails as they moved.
30

Lorenz and a team of investigators believe that a combination of forces may work to rearrange Racetrack Playa's rocks. "We saw that it would take a lot of wind to move these rocks, which are larger than you'd expect
35 wind to move," Lorenz explains. "That led us to this idea that ice might be picking up the rocks and floating them." As they explained in the January issue of *The American Journal of Physics*, instead of moving along with wind-driven sheets of ice, the rocks may instead be lifted by the
40 ice, making them more subject to the wind's force. The key, Lorenz says, is that the lifting by an "ice collar" reduces friction with the ground, to the point that the wind now has enough force to move the rock. The rock moves, the ice doesn't, and because part of the rock juts through
45 the ice, it marks the territory it has covered.

Lorenz's team came to its conclusion through a combination of intuition, lab work, and observation—not that the last part was easy. Watching the rocks travel is a bit like witnessing the rusting of a hubcap. Instances of
50 movement are rare and last for only a few seconds.

Lorenz's team placed low-resolution cameras on the cliffs (which are about 30 miles from the nearest paved road) to take pictures once per hour. For the past three winters, the
55 researchers have weathered extreme temperatures and several flat tires to measure how often the thermometer dips below freezing, how often the playa gets rain and floods, and the strength of the winds. "The measurements seem to back up our hypothesis," he says. "Any of the
60 theories may be true at any one time, but ice rafting may be the best explanation for the trails we've been seeing. We've seen trails like this documented in Arctic coastal areas, and the mechanism is somewhat similar. A belt of ice surrounds a boulder during high tide, picks it up, and
65 then drops it elsewhere."

His "ice raft theory" was also borne out by an experiment that used the ingenuity of a high school science fair. Lorenz placed a basalt pebble in a
70 Tupperware container with water so that the pebble projected just above the surface. He then turned the container upside down in a baking tray filled with a layer of coarse sand at its base, and put the whole thing in his home freezer. The rock's "keel" (its protruding part)
75 projected downward into the sand, which simulated the cracked surface of the playa (which scientists call "Special K" because of its resemblance to cereal flakes). A gentle push or slight puff of air caused the Tupperware container to move, just as an ice raft would under the right
80 conditions. The pebble made a trail in the soft sand. "It was primitive but effective," Lorenz says of the experiment.

Lorenz has spent the last 20 years studying Titan, a
85 moon of Saturn. He says that Racetrack Playa's surface mirrors that of a dried lakebed on Titan. Observations and experiments on Earth may yield clues to that moon's geology. "We also may get some idea of how climate affects geology—particularly as the climate changes here
90 on Earth," Lorenz says. "When we study other planets and their moons, we're forced to use Occam's razor—sometimes the simplest answer is best, which means you look to Earth for some answers. Once you get out there on Earth, you realize how strange so much of its surface is.
95 So, you have to figure there's weird stuff to be found on Titan as well."

Whether that's true or not will take much more investigation, he adds: "One day, we'll figure all this out.
100 For the moment, the moving rocks present a wonderful problem to study in a beautiful place."

31. Which of the following best describes the content of this passage?

   A. A discussion of how Ralph Lorenz's research on basalt rocks compares with the work of other scientists.
   B. A systematic refutation of the claim that winds play a role in moving rocks in Death Valley.
   C. A description of how one scientist led a team of researchers in an attempt to solve a longstanding scientific puzzle.
   D. An exploration of how, over the last six decades, various groups of scientists have explained the movement of the Racetrack Playa rocks.

32. The author mentions a "hubcap" in the fifth paragraph (lines 47-65) primarily to support the idea that:

   F. some of the rocks in Death Valley National Park are as heavy as automobiles.
   G. rocks can move over great distances when they are shaped like wheels.
   H. Lorenz placed his team in great danger by allowing them to gather data in extreme weather.
   J. the process of observing the rocks move was extremely slow and difficult.

33. Ralph Lorenz's attitude toward solving the mystery discussed in the passage can best be described as:

   A. apprehensive and uncertain.
   B. confident and optimistic.
   C. scornful and cynical.
   D. proud and amused.

34. In the seventh paragraph (lines 84-96), the discussion of Titan most nearly suggests that:

   F. Earth and Saturn most likely formed at around the same time.
   G. changes in temperature create similar geological effects on different planets and moons.
   H. scientists have traditionally overestimated the Earth's uniqueness.
   J. studying Titan can reveal important information about how the Earth's moon was formed.

35. As it is used in line 20, the word *holds* most nearly means:

   A. argues.
   B. carries.
   C. limits.
   D. grasps.

36. Which of the following best summarizes Lorenz's hypothesis about how the Racetrack Playa rocks move across the valley floor?

   F. They are carried along by wind-driven sheets of ice.
   G. They are pushed by the heat generated from friction with the ground.
   H. They are lifted by "ice collars," then pushed by the wind.
   J. They glide on air currents that develop during rainstorms.

37. In context of the passage, the phrase "But neither theory is rock solid" is most likely intended to:

   A. explain why strong winds do not develop at Racetrack Playa.
   B. provide a humorous commentary on the shortcomings of two existing explanations.
   C. criticize the scientific community for failing to investigate why the rocks moved.
   D. suggest that modern science is fundamentally limited.

38. It can be reasonably inferred from the passage that the winds at Racetrack Playa:

   F. create sailing ice.
   G. do not play a role in moving rocks along the valley floor.
   H. form trails in the valley's surface.
   J. blow at less than 100 miles per hour.

39. The passage suggests that the experiment Lorenz designed to test his hypothesis:

   A. was effective in spite of its crude construction.
   B. revealed important similarities between Earth and Titan.
   C. conclusively determined the forces behind the rocks' movement.
   D. demonstrated the unique properties of basalt.

40. The passage indicates that the most convincing explanation for how and why the rocks in Death Valley National Park move is known as:

   F. the "ice sailing theory."
   G. the "ice raft theory."
   H. the "ice collar theory."
   J. Occam's razor.

Answers and Explanations

Prose Fiction

1. B

Consider the context of Lau Po's statement: Waverly asks Lau Po to play with her, and he smiles at her and then evidently agrees to a game. We know this because she states that he *turned out to be a much better player than [her] brothers.* So his attitude is positive, and he wants to play. On that basis, you can clearly eliminate (D), and (A) and (C) also don't make a whole lot of sense. (B) is consistent with the scenario in the passage: he's an old man, and Waverly is a young girl – he refers to her as "little sister." Logically, he must be saying that he hasn't played chess with anyone so much younger than himself in a long time.

2. G

This question requires less thought than might be initially obvious. The key is to notice that the bulk of the paragraph is comprised of a list of the "secrets" that Lau Po teaches Waverly; even though there is other information in the paragraph, it is not the focus. (F) is incorrect because Waverly never says that she felt disappointed; (H) is incorrect because the passage never states that Waverly kept her games with Lau Po secret; and in (J), even though Waverly does imply that she and Lau Po played for Life Savers, that is a minor point.

3. B

(B) is correct because even though Waverly's mother doesn't know much about chess, her argument is hard to refute: the fact that Waverly lost fewer pieces during her second tournament *would* seem to indicate that she played a better game. For (A), there is no evidence in the passage that Waverly often found it difficult to speak in her mother's presence – there's only evidence that her mother hears what she wants to hear, which isn't the same thing. (C) is flat-out incorrect – Waverly knows much more about chess than her mother; and (D) is simply off topic. There's no information to indicate what language Waverly spoke to her mother in.

4. H

The key word in the question is **first** – the question is only asking about Waverly's initial reaction to the suggestion that she compete in a tournament. You need to make sure to start from the place where the tournament is first mentioned, so scan for the word *tournament* until you find it in the topic sentence of seventh paragraph (lines 45-46) and then read the following information slowly. What does the passage say? *I desperately wanted to go, but I bit back my tongue.* In other words, she kept quiet. Waverly's mother is the one who smiles, so (F) is out. (G) is completely wrong: Waverly never pleads to attend. Careful with (J): Waverly does suggest that she might lose if she competed in a tournament, but she only does so **later**, as she and her mother are walking home.

5. D

Consider the context: the passages states that *the boy disappeared...and I saw only my white pieces and his black ones waiting on the other side.* So logically, *ran out of* must mean something like "disappeared." That is the definition of *vanished*, so (D) is correct.

6. F

The key word is *sandbox*, so you want to start by scanning for it. It shows up in line 33, where the passage states *Never hurl pieces into the sandbox after you have lost a game, because then you must find them again, by yourself, after apologizing to all around you.* (F) is thus the only possible answer.

7. C

Remember that the question asks about what the passage *suggests*, not what the passage *says*. Think also about how the answers are presented: two state that Waverly's mother's humility is genuine, and two state that it is false. In other words, the question is asking you whether the passage should be taken literally. This is an important point because whenever ACT questions ask you whether a word or phrase should be understood literally, the answer is typically "no." If those words or phrases were intended literally, there would be no reason to ask the question in the first place. You can therefore start by assuming that (A) and (B) are incorrect. In this case, the fact that Waverly's mother *proudly* watches her daughter repeatedly and publicly defeat her opponents implies that she knows her daughter's success is due to skill, practice, and talent, not luck. (C) is therefore correct. In (D), there is no information to directly suggest that Waverly is becoming arrogant.

8. F

If you're not sure about the phrase *fine points* from the sentence in which it appears, keep reading. The rest of the paragraph is devoted to discussing proper chess behavior; it clearly describes what players should and should not do. The phrase *fine points* must therefore refer to those specific behaviors, making (F) correct. There is no information in the passage that would support (G), (H), or (J).

9. A

In order to answer this question correctly, you must understand that Waverly is manipulating her mother by employing reverse psychology. Waverly's mother clearly takes great pride in her daughter's chess-playing ability, and she also does not want Waverly to doubt those abilities or her potential to succeed in an American context. At the same time, though, she is suspicious of (American) strangers and hesitant to allow her daughter to interact with them. Waverly is acutely aware of her mother's ambivalence but is betting on the fact that her mother is more invested in having her daughter maintain a strong belief in her ability to succeed than she is in protecting her daughter from the outside world. When Waverly states that she might *bring shame on her family*, she is assuming that her mother will be so upset by Waverly's belief she might fail that she will relent and allow her to participate in the tournament.

10. J

Waverly's mother clearly wants to hold onto her Chinese culture: she ascribes her daughter's success in chess to "luck" with *proper Chinese humility* (line 43); she is hesitant to allow Waverly to compete against American strangers; and she gives Waverly a *chang* – a red jade tablet – for luck before her first tournament. At the same time, though, she clearly has her own ideas about things: in the last part of the passage, she holds firm to the idea that Waverly should focus on losing fewer pieces, even though

Waverly insists that the number of pieces she loses is irrelevant to her success. In (F), Waverly's mother obviously supports her daughter, but she does so in an understated, (falsely) humble way. She doesn't cheer her on or express excitement. (H) goes too far in the other direction; although Waverly's mother holds her daughter to a high standard, she is also encouraging and does not look down on her daughter. (G) is off topic; there is nothing in the passage to suggest that Waverly's mother is either simple or naïve.

Social Science

11. C

The key word is *longevity*, so start by scanning Passage A for it. You'll find it in line 11. The sentence in which it appears states that *psychosocial factors such as stress are the single most important variable in determining length of life*. In other words, all other factors – including genetics – are *less* important. That is exactly what (C) says. Be careful with (A): it sounds entirely logical but is not actually supported by the passage. (B) runs counter to both the passage and common sense: individual behaviors such as smoking obviously do matter. (D) is off-topic: the passage mentions adult-onset diabetes, but only in relation to stress. It says nothing about diabetes and longevity.

12. F

There's no real shortcut or key word for this question, but the passage is short enough that you can find the information quickly enough if you focus on the list of diseased correlated with stress. (Make sure not get distracted by the word *effects* in in line 18, though; that paragraph is not the only place information about the effects of stress appears.) The answer is found in line 9, which indicates that stress "atrophies" (weakens) muscles. (G) says exactly the opposite of what the passage states: line 20 indicates that antibiotics become *less* effective as a result of stress. (H) is incorrect because the passage only mentions genetics as a risk factor in disease; it says nothing about whether stress effects a person's genome. (J) is incorrect because the passage says nothing about stress making patients *ineligible* for surgery.

13. B

The quotation focuses on the fact that surgery is of limited value in the long-term if a person continues to experience significant amounts of stress. Basically, it's used to support the point that stress is the most important factor in the ability to become/stay healthy – more important than medication, genetics, etc. In other words, stress has a "disproportionate" impact on health, which is what (B) says. (A) is incorrect because the passage only mentions one type of surgery, and the focus is on long-term health, not short-term fixes. The point is also not that the surgery itself is ineffective, but that stress makes it less effective in the long term. (C) is incorrect because the passage says nothing about delaying surgery, for severely ill patients or any other patients. (D) is incorrect because again, the focus is on the effect of stress on stent surgery. The passage says nothing about whether the benefits of stent surgery have been overestimated.

14. G

Consider the context of the phrase: the author is introducing the fact that certain types of stress can be beneficial. In addition, the phrase *take heart* itself means "don't worry." The only answer that fits is (G). Playing process of elimination, (F) is negative and can be crossed out. Careful with (H): the passage states that small amounts of *some types* of stress ("good," "tolerable") can lead to a sense of exhilaration. It says nothing about *toxic* stress being anything other than toxic. (J) is incorrect because it is entirely unsupported by the passage.

15. D

Be careful with (A). The writer certainly suggests that stress is a serious problem among the people surveyed, but the idea that it constitutes an impending (about to occur) crisis is too extreme to be consistent with the passage. Careful with (B) also: the first paragraph does indicate that teenagers and young adult are more stressed than before, but that paragraph does not actually *describe* the effects of stress on those groups. The only description of chronic stress comes two paragraphs later. (C) may be factually true, but it is also entirely unsupported by the passage. (D) is correct because the first paragraph indicates that stress is rampant among teens, young adults, and adults, i.e., *a range of groups*.

16. A

You can start by looking for Robert Sapolsky's name, but in this case, *1970s* is a more efficient key term to focus on because Sapolsky's name appears multiple times in the passage whereas 1970s only appears once. What information does the passage provide about Sapolsky's research in the 1970s? It was responsible for the discovery that hormones, including cortisol, released during the fight-or-flight response can cause significant harm in the long term. Logically, then, researchers were unaware of the connection between harm to the body and long-term exposure to fight-or-flight hormones such as cortisol prior to the 1970s – and that is what (A) says. (B) is incorrect because the passage does not imply that researchers did not know how fight-or-flight hormones helped human beings in the past. (C) is incorrect because the passage does not indicate that researchers actively questioned the relationship between toxic stress and harm to the body. This answer could be true, but the passage does not explicitly support it. Careful with (D): again, the passage only indicates that researchers were unaware of the harmful effects of chronic exposure to cortisol. It does not imply that they were unaware that cortisol was involved in the fight-or-flight response.

17. J

In line 59, the word *paints* is used figuratively to mean "indicates" or "reveals" – there is no artistic connotation. *Scale, struggling,* and *released* are all used literally.

18. H

This question is actually much more straightforward than it might initially seem. If you scan the two passages (or remember them well enough), Robert Sapolsky's name appears in both. Robert Sapolsky = *a key figure in the field of stress research*. (F) is far too broad – the passages focus only on stress research, not on science as a whole. (G) applies to Passage B but not Passage A, which only mentions the effects of stress on bones and muscles. (J) is incorrect because only Passage B mentions cortisol.

19. B

If you've noted the key difference between the passages, you can use the big picture to answer this question without rereading anything. To sum up, Passage A focuses exclusively on the negative aspects of stress, whereas Passage B also discusses some positive aspects. That makes (B) the only possible answer. (A) and (D) are discussed only in Passage A, and (C) is discussed in both passages.

20. H

Although this may seem like an enormously complicated question, it can actually be answered with information from only Passage B. Start by defining the findings from passage B. The key is to focus on the end of that passage; the phrase *recent research* in line 58 is a clue that the information is in the last paragraph. The last sentence – often the most important sentence of a passage – indicates that worrying about worrying is bad for you. The logical advice for surgical patients, then, would be to avoid that kind of worry, i.e., *dwelling on their anxieties*. If you need to confirm that the surgical patients in Passage A are ones whose conditions would be exacerbated by stress, you can check it out, but it is not actually necessary to reread the portion of Passage A that discusses them. None of the other answers is directly supported by Passage B.

Humanities

21. C

In paragraph 5 (lines 33-43), the author states that *Emerson derived many of his own insights from the German intellectuals Johann Goethe and Immanuel Kant, and he was also an avid student of Eastern religion*, eliminating (A), (B), and (D). The opening sentence indicates that "The American Scholar" was a speech given by Emerson himself.

22. G

This is an inference question, which means that the answer is not explicitly stated in the passage. To answer it, you must consider what the passage does state, then determine what can be directly inferred from it. First, though, you need to find the information. The key phrase in the question is "home life" – the passage focuses on Emerson's writing, so you know that the discussion of this idea will be limited. Although the words *home* and *life* do not appear next to one another in the passage, the sixth paragraph indicates that *Emerson's life…seemed placid when compared with the lives of many other writers, it is perhaps because his home thrived on order and unassuming routine…* If you're not sure what *placid* (peaceful) or *unassuming* (modest) means, focus on the part that is absolutely clear: Emerson's home *thrived on order*. Since Emerson is being compared to "other writers," the other writers must have been the opposite. What's the opposite of orderly and peaceful? Chaotic or *exciting*. (G) is the answer that fits the necessary idea most closely.

23. A

To find the necessary information, you need to scan the passage for the date *2010*. It appears in line 69, where the author states that in 2010, Lopate was *prompted to take a look at a writer who had previously left him cold*. What does it mean to be *left cold*? In this case, to be unaffected emotionally. That idea is further supported by Lopate's statement that Emerson's essays *sounded oracular, abstract, dizzyingly inspired, like visionary sermons: the thinking and language spectacular, the man somehow missing*. So basically, Lopate felt as if he couldn't perceive an actual person behind the words. (A) is the answer that directly captures that idea.

24. F

Start by scanning the passage for the key phrase "literary canon." You'll find it in line 54, where the author states that *Emerson has become an afterthought in the American literary canon because he lacks that outsider romance of our other mid-nineteenth century giants*. That corresponds to (F). The passage does not directly support (G) or (H), and (J) directly contradicts the passage.

25. C

The phrase in question is highly metaphorical, so you need to look at the surrounding information to understand its literal meaning. The author indicates that he had an extremely positive reaction to his initial encounter with Emerson – he identified with Emerson's questioning of convention and decided to attend college and ultimately become a writer. Aside from the fact that (C) captures the meaning of the phrase, it can also be chosen by process of elimination because it is the only positive answer.

26. G

The question asks you about Scott Russell Sanders, so start by looking for his name. If you don't remember where it is, scan topic sentences – the name doesn't appear until line 79, so that's the most efficient way of finding it. That sentence also is where the author states the answer directly: *Like Lopate, contemporary nature essayist Scott Russell Sanders thinks that Emerson's most appealing presence rests not in his essays, but in his journals.* (G) is thus correct.

27. A

Start by looking for the key phrase: "English and European thinking." It's in line 37, so you need to read from there. Note that you need to go all the way to the end of the paragraph to find the answer; the fact that the last sentence starts with *but* is a clue that it's important. So what does the passage tell us about Emerson's attitude toward English and European thinking – it was pretty positive (he was influenced by Kant and Goethe) but not overwhelmingly so. (D) is extremely negative, so you can eliminate it on those grounds, and (C) is somewhat negative as well (it's also entirely unsupported by the passage – the author only says that *Emerson* was influenced by those thinkers; he says nothing to suggest that *English and European thinking* were too reliant on them). Now you need to consider the second piece of information: *But Emerson argued that all ideas should be tested by individual experience, and not merely accepted based on the power of precedent.* In other words, even though he thought English and European thinking were valuable, he also thought that people should make up their own minds, based on their individual experiences – which is what (A) says. For (B), the passage never states that Emerson believed English and European thinking *could not* be applied to life in the U.S. In addition, the answer is phrased in an absolute manner, suggesting that it is incorrect.

28. H

It's reasonable to start off by reading the first sentence of this paragraph, but unfortunately it won't get you to the answer on this particular question. It only tells us that the paragraph will compare Emerson to other writers in some way. This is where you need to be careful: the paragraph discusses Emerson's home life, *not* his literary style.

In fact, it does not mention his style at all. So (G) is incorrect. (F) also doesn't work: the paragraph never directly compares Emerson's public and private lives. And (J) is the opposite of what the passage says: Emerson *lacked* the outsider romance of his contemporaries. (H) correctly identifies the paragraph's function, even if it does so from an angle you are not expecting. The discussion of Emerson's home life is included to explain why Emerson *has become an afterthought in the American literary canon* – in other words, why he's not as popular as some other American writers.

29. D

Start by considering the context. The passage states that Emerson *urged [his listeners] to do their own thinking instead of using imported ideas from the Old World.* The next sentence, however, qualifies that idea by indicating that Emerson was influenced by ideas from German intellectuals (i.e., the "Old World"). In other words, he didn't think those ideas were completely bad. So *uniformly* must mean something like "completely" or "always." That is the definition of *invariably*, so (D) is correct.

30. F

The question asks about Emerson's *essays*, so be careful to look only for information about his essays – not his journals. If you get confused, you could end up with an answer that says exactly the opposite of what you want. What do we know about Emerson's essays relative to his journals? They were a lot less personal and a lot harder to relate to (remember from #6 that Sanders believed Emerson's most appealing writing was found in his journals). Lopate states that Emerson's essays *sounded oracular, abstract, dizzyingly inspired, like visionary sermons,* and Sanders states that *[Emerson] seemed too high-flown, too cocksure, too earnest.* The words *oracular, dizzyingly inspired,* and *high-flown* are synonyms for *lofty* and *exalted,* making (F) correct. (G) is simply off-topic; (H) and (J) are the opposite of what you want (*cocksure* is the opposite of *tentative,* and *personal* is the opposite of *impersonal* (line 73).

Natural Science

31. C

This is a very straightforward question, so the primary challenge is locating the information. The key phrase in the question is *generate heat*, so you're going to look for it. Unfortunately, the passage is quite dense, and the question doesn't provide much giveaway in terms of where the answer is likely to be located. If you're not sure where to start, scan the passage for those words while dragging your finger down the page. You'll find them in line 30, which states that *the rest [of the bees] are just hanging there, tensing their flight muscles to generate heat.* The only major clue is the dash in line 29. Ideally, you should have circled it when you skimmed through the passage initially because important information is often located next to dashes.

32. G

There are two clues in this question: first, the question asks about the Mink Hollow hives, so you know that's your key phrase, and second, it asks about the *first* hives, so you know the answer is going to be at the beginning of the discussion about Mink Hollow. If you scan topic sentences, you'll find the first mention of Mink Hollow in line 54. The sentence states that Esais started the apiary with *a trio of hand-me-down hives.* The phrase *hand-me-down* means that the hives didn't originally belong to Esaias; logically, they must have been owned by another bee-keeper (who else would keep bee hives?), so the answer is (G). (F) is incorrect because Esais's hive is described as being the size of a soccer ball when he speaks to the author of the passage, not when he first started the apiary; (H) is incorrect because the passage indicates that the hives were originally most productive in *late* May; and (J) is incorrect because the passage says nothing about the bees being nervous.

33. C

The passage only tells us that Esais was trained as a scientist and describes his experience starting the apiary; it never tells us why he chose to become a beekeeper. (A) is incorrect because lines 61-62 state that bees began disappearing in 2006; (B) is incorrect because line 12 states that the honey bee is also known as *Apis mellifera*; and (D) is incorrect because the second paragraph discusses the hives' winter activity and indicates that they can survive as far north as Alaska.

34. F

Think about the context: the passage is talking about the *maximum* amount of nectar that the bees collect. In that context, *increases* is the only word that fits. *Stings* is a word commonly associated with bees, but it does not make sense in context, and neither *developments* nor *exaggerations* is consistent with the idea of the bees' nectar yield rising.

35. B

The information you need is located in the first paragraph, so even if you don't remember where it's located, you can find it pretty quickly if you start at the beginning. The paragraph indicates that Esaias uses a cast-iron scale, an instrument that's been around since the 1800s (old technology), as well as a laptop and 12-bit recorder (new technology). (A) is incorrect because the passage never states any of his instruments were developed for bee-keepers; (C) makes no sense in context; and (D) is incorrect because the passage states that Esais uses an old-fashioned scale, not a digital one. Don't get fooled by the references to the laptop and data logger: they *could* contain digital elements, but the question asks specifically about the scale.

36. J

An epiphany is a breakthrough or revelation, and the key to this question is to understand that the "epiphany" refers to the situation discussed at the end of the *previous* paragraph. If you start reading in line 77 and continue down, you'll get lost – the final paragraph only discusses the consequences of Esais's realization, not the realization itself. What does the end of the previous paragraph describe? The fact that Esais looked at his graphs and realized that the moment when the bees were collecting the largest amount of nectar had shifted from late May to Mid-May – a two-week shift. The answer is therefore (J).

37. B

The passage only states that scale hives allow beekeepers to detect whether robber bees have entered a hive – it says nothing about determining *when* they will do so. (A) and (C) are mentioned in lines 39-41 (*a beekeeper can...storage*), and (D) is discussed in lines 43-48 (*A graph...pollination*).

38. F

Remember that when you encounter a paragraph-function question and see an answer choice that refers to a shift in focus, you should check that answer first. In this case, zeroing in on (F) and then double-checking it in the passage may be the most efficient way of answering the question. Unfortunately, reading the beginning of the paragraph won't work here. The real topic – the emergence of CCD – isn't introduced until line 61. You can still get the correct answer by reading the entire paragraph, but working this way will take more time. (G) is incorrect because the passage never explains what inspired Esaias to start the apiary; (H) is incorrect because the passage does not actually *describe* the pollination process; and (J) is incorrect because the passage states that there is no explanation for CCD – there is nothing to refute.

39. C

Remember that answers to inference questions, especially ones involving numbers, do not usually appear directly in the passage, and that you'll probably have to do some basic calculations. Hive weights get discussed a fair amount in the passage, so you want to think carefully about key words before you go back to the passage. Most of the passage talks about nectar-collecting in the spring and summer, but the question asks about January, so that word is likely to appear only near the answer. If you scan topic sentences, you'll find it in line 18. That sentence states that the colony weighed 94.5 lbs in January but that the weight can rise to 275 lbs by July. That's a difference of 180 lbs, making (C) the answer. Again, note that 180 is the only number among the answer choices that does not appear in the passage.

40. J

Careful with this question – locating the date *1992* won't give you sufficient information to answer the question. You'll have to go through a few steps of reasoning. The passage states that Esais started his apiary in 1992, and that after the 2006 season, he realized that over the past fifteen years the bees' peak nectar-collecting time had shifted from mid-May to late May. That means, when Esais started the apiary in 1992, the bees were collecting the largest amount of nectar in late May.

Prose Fiction

1. C

The information necessary to answer the question is located in lines 32-37. If you do not remember where the narrator's motivation for taking the drum is discussed, the most efficient way to find it is to recognize that you are looking for an explanation – the word *reasons* in line 37 indicates that an explanation is being given. Because the phrase *similar reasons* refers to information that has just been discussed, you must back up and read the previous paragraph. What information does it reveal? Elsie wanted the earrings because they made her feel as if she *was part of [Curtis's] work*. In other words, she felt personally connected to them. The narrator's statement that she *took the drum for similar reasons* thus means that her theft was motivated by a sense of personal connection. (A) is incorrect because there is no mention of the drum's value – Elsie only states that *it wasn't that the earrings were so valuable*. Careful with (B): Elsie does propose that the narrator *claim* she took the drum in order to have it repaired, but that is not why the narrator actually took the drum. In (D), the narrator does say that *later [she'll] find its rightful owner*, but again, that was not her reason for taking the drum.

2. J

You should be able to eliminate (F) pretty easily; Elsie wants the narrator to return the drum, but it clearly does not belong to Elsie. At this point, it makes sense to scan the passage for each name. Note that the fastest way to answer the question is not to go in order of the answers but rather to check the names in the order in which they appear in the passage. Since the correct owner, Jewett Parker Tatro, is mentioned first (in line 65-72 and again in 99-103), you will not have to check the other answers. If you have difficulty figuring out that Tatro owned the drum from the passage – the author does not directly state that he was the owner but rather leaves the reader to infer it by mentioning the drum in context of his "hoard" (line 101) – you can play process of elimination. In the last paragraph, the Elsie indicates that she wants to talk to Old Shaawano and Mrs. String because they are likely to know something about the drum's origins, not because the drum belonged to them.

3. B

The fact that *compromised* normally means "came to an agreement" should immediately tell you that (D) is incorrect – right answers to vocabulary-in-context questions virtually never restate the most common meaning. Now think about the context: the narrator feels bad about the fact that Elsie could be implicated in her theft, and states that Elsie's reputation is also "at stake." In this context, "inquired about" does not make sense, and "condemned" is far too strong. Only "put at risk" is consistent with the idea that the narrator's theft *could* get Elsie in trouble.

4. F

Remember that this is an inference question, which means that the answer won't be stated directly in the passage. First, let's consider what we know about Elsie and the earrings: she had the opportunity to steal them but chose to be honest, purchasing them instead. She also tells us that the earrings appeared in a famous photograph, implying that they could be worth a lot of money. The narrator then asks Elsie whether she revealed that the earrings had appeared in the photograph before she bought them – in other words, she wants to know just how honest Elsie actually was about the earrings' value. If Elsie had revealed that they earrings were in the photograph, she could have had to pay a lot of money for them; however, her response in lines 79-80 directly implies that she did not reveal that information, making (F) correct. (G) is completely off-topic; (H) is the opposite of the truth – Elsie was well aware of the earrings' value, which is why she did not mention that they were in the photograph; and (J) is incorrect because the passage says nothing to indicate that Elsie was embarrassed.

5. C

This is a literal comprehension question, so start by scanning for the key word *argument*. You won't find *argument*, but you will find *arguing* in line 88, which is where you need to look to answer the question. What information do we get there? Elsie shuts her mouth tightly and *This is as angry as we ever get* (i.e., not very angry =mild)*, and we both know it won't last* (=short-lived). So (C) is correct.

6. J

Although this is an inference question, it is a relatively straightforward one, provided that you back up and read the entire sentence in which the line reference appears. The key is the information between the parentheses. The narrator states that she'll consider returning the drum because she knows Elsie "won't hold her to" her offer to return it – i.e., that she won't be required to keep her word. So (J) is correct. (F), (G), and (H) all contain ideas mentioned in the passage, but none of those answers correctly answers the question asked.

7. A

If you don't remember where Satie is mentioned, start scanning from the very beginning of the passage; you'll find his name immediately, in line 3. As is true for #6, this is a very straightforward question if you back up and read the sentence before. It states the Elsie *likes to sit and listen to music*, directly implying that Satie is the name of the person whose music she is listening to. (A) is the only answer choice consistent with that idea.

8. G

The most efficient way to answer this question is to read the end of the previous paragraph and the beginning of the one in question. (G) is correct because the latter continues the idea begun in the previous paragraph, namely that that the narrator and Elsie never stayed angry for long. The paragraph in question opens with an illustration of that idea: the next morning, not only is Elsie no longer angry at the narrator's refusal to return the drum but she is also eager to discover where it came from. If you choose to start by reading through the answer choices, don't eliminate anything before you've actually thought through what it says. If you jump to cross out answers, it is very likely you'll get rid of the correct one since it does not actually mention information that appears in the paragraph. (F) is incorrect because although the narrator does mention the Tatro family, she does not discuss her relationship with them; (H) is incorrect because the narrator only states that Elsie wants to discover the drum's origins – it says nothing about how they went about it; and (J) is incorrect because it is the narrator who stole the drum; the paragraph makes no mention of the Ojibwe.

9. A

This question requires you to make a somewhat bigger leap than most of the other inference questions in this set. The key is the dialogue between the narrator and Elsie beginning in line19. Elsie states that she left the earrings in *on purpose*, implying that she wanted the narrator to notice them. Why did she want the narrator to notice them? So that she can point out (=call attention to) the fact that she, unlike the narrator, acted honestly and purchased an item that she had the opportunity to steal. Essentially, she's trying to guilt-trip the narrator into returning the drum. Only (A) is consistent with that idea.

10. G

The easiest way to approach this question is to play positive/negative. For the first three-quarters of the passage, Elsie is upset that the narrator does not want to return the drum (negative). Eliminate (H) because *curiosity* is somewhat positive. Starting in line 91, however, her attitude becomes much more positive. Eliminate (F) because *indifference* is negative. Both *dismay* and *skepticism* work for the first word, but (J) is incorrect because *reverence*, although positive, is far too strong. Elsie is enthusiastic about finding the drum's origins, but she is not actually in awe.

Social Science

11. D

Although the answer is stated more or less in the passage, this is actually more of a main point question. If you understand the gist of the passage, you shouldn't find it necessary to look back. What's the author's point? That unlike other people, who think *in a combination of words and vague, generalized pictures*, she thinks in images alone and uses them to build more generalized concepts. That information by itself is enough to give you (D). If you're not sure, the most effective way to approach the question to scan topic sentences; the answer is located in the topic sentence of the fourth paragraph (lines 37-39): *Unlike those of most people, my thoughts move from video-like, specific images to generalizations and concepts.*

12. F

The author discusses David in the last paragraph, so that's where you want to focus. What does she reveal? That David was able to complete his drawings "effortlessly," but that she had to spend *many hours copying and photographing them in [her] memory.* Therefore, in comparison to David, she had to exert much more effort, and the answer must be (F). (G) is exactly the opposite of what the author implies, and (H) and (J) are simply off topic.

13. C

Look for the key word *Great Danes*, which appears in the fourth paragraph (lines 43-44). In back-to-back sentences, the author states that Helga, her aunt's dog, and the Fitwell advertisement (i.e., a media image) all contributed to her concept of what made a dog a Great Dane. Although computer graphics are mentioned in the next paragraph, they are not mentioned as contributing to the author's idea of a Great Dane, so (C) is incorrect.

14. F

Don't be fooled by the fact that the question asks about a "renowned" scientist. If you don't look back to the passage, you might assume that the author would have a positive response; however, the author states that she viewed his work as "ridiculous" (line 15) – a negative reaction. That eliminates both (G) and (H). *Resignation* (passive, unhappy acceptance) makes no sense in context. *Scorn*, however, is consistent with the idea of ridiculousness, so (F) is correct.

15. B

Remember that this is an inference question, so the answer will not be stated directly in the passage. Start by looking for the word *steeple* – it's italicized, making it relatively easy to spot (ideally, you should have circled it as you read through the passage – italicized words are almost always important). The author gives us two pieces of information: first, that many people think of a steeple by picturing a generic steeple rather than one attached to a specific building; and second, that she starts by picturing specific images and then working up to general concepts. As a result, it's logical to assume that if asked to imagine a steeple, she would think of all the specific steeples she had seen. (A) is exactly the opposite of what you want, and (C) and (D) are both off topic. Even if you don't know the definition of *amalgam*, don't get thrown off by it; the other answers don't fit, and the rest of (B) is consistent with the idea you want.

16. J

Start by looking for the phrase *people with autism* – most of the passage focuses specifically on the author, so you're looking for a place where she doesn't talk about herself. If you know that she spends the first few paragraph focusing almost exclusively how she thinks in relation to more verbally-oriented people, you can assume that the information you're looking for will not be located there. In addition, the word *I* appears constantly in those paragraphs, suggesting that the focus is on the author alone. Otherwise, if you skim topic sentences, you'll find the necessary phrase in line 55; if you read that paragraph carefully, you'll find the information you need to answer the question (although not the answer itself – remember that the question asks what the author *suggests*). What does the author tell us? That *not all people with autism are highly visual thinkers*, and that *People throughout the world are on a continuum of visualization skills*. In other words, people with autism are no more or less likely to be exclusively visual than anyone else, hence (J). (F) is incorrect because the author says nothing about extreme visual orientation being highly unusual in people with autism, only that not all people with autism are highly visual; (G) is completely off topic; and (H) is incorrect because the author says nothing about extreme visual orientation being *more* common among people with autism.

17. A

Consider the context: the author is describing how she *copied* David's drawing style, so logically, *emulate* must mean something like "copy." That is the definition of *mimic*, so (A) is correct. The other words do not make sense in context.

18. H

The key to this question is the first sentence. The topic sentence, *It wasn't until I went to college that I realized some people are completely verbal and think only in words*, directly implies that the author will spend the rest of the passage describing that discovery –

and in fact, she goes on to do just that (*I first suspected this when I read an article…*). (F) is too extreme: the author only indicates that she thought the one particular study was "ridiculous," not that all scientific research was that way; in (G), the author mentions that she invents things but does not actually describe the process she uses to do so; and in (J), the author only indicates that she did not agree with the "renowned scientist" – she does not compare or contrast her research to his.

19. B

In the first paragraph, the author cites Galton, who contrasts people who *see vivid mental pictures* with those with "low pictorial imagery" – people who could *remember their breakfast table but…not see it*. It is therefore possible to infer that people who with low pictorial imagery are those that do not "see vivid mental pictures." (B) is therefore correct. (C) is the opposite of what you what, and (A) and (D) are off topic.

20. D

The question is phrased a very general way, one that doesn't give you any immediate clues as to where the answer might be located, so you might want to use the answer choices to give you some direction. (A) and (B) don't necessarily help, but both (C) and (D) both deal with time, suggesting that the correct answer might have something to do with it. When you go back to the passage to scan, you might therefore want to look for phrases involving time. Unfortunately, there's no real shortcut to this question – the answer is located in neither a first nor a last sentence. Instead, it's in the middle of the fourth paragraph (line 51), where the author states directly that her memories occur *in strict chronological order*. That makes (D) the only possible answer.

Humanities

21. C

The first paragraph presents context for the rest of the passage. It describes an ancient (i.e., longstanding) argument (i.e., a debate) about fiction: some people view it as positive, BUT others see it as negative. That directly corresponds to (C). (A) and (B) both take ideas discussed presented in the passage and rephrase them from an incorrect angle:

the first paragraph does mentions that some people have believed that stories *cultivate our...mental development*, but the *purpose* of the paragraph is not to make that argument. (B) is incorrect because the author is presenting a debate in a neutral manner, not making criticism. In addition, the focus is on fiction, not the media. (D) is incorrect because the passage only states that the debate over fiction is "ancient" – there is no description of how fiction developed from ancient times.

22. H

Consider the context: the author is discussing why people are *not* moved by non-fiction arguments – that is, arguments based on *argument and evidence* (line 32). The phrase *critical and skeptical* in line 34 also essentially defines the phrase *with our shields up*. That information is only directly consistent with (H). (F) and (J) refer to exactly the opposite: the sense of connection and empathy provoked by reading fiction. (G) is off-topic and irrelevant to the passage.

23. B

The key word is *traditionally*. The second paragraph provides historical context, so that is where you want to focus. The examples of Plato and Newton Minow both support the idea that fiction is harmful to society, as well as the statement *They are not in the public interest* (line 20). The other answers are not supported by the passage.

24. H

The first two paragraphs of Passage A are essentially introductory, providing (historical) context for he discussion about fiction. The author does not actually begin to offer his own thoughts until line 22, as indicated by the phrase *But recently...* As a result, you can assume that the answer is somewhere in paragraphs three through five. You can use the big picture to eliminate (G) immediately – it's exactly the opposite of the point of the passage. *Non-fiction* is what makes people "critical and skeptical." (F) is off-topic: the passage says nothing about fiction reflecting social or political controversies. Be careful with (J). The passage only indicates that readers of fiction are likely to believe *one* particular lie: namely, that the world is more just than it actually is. It says nothing about making readers trust people more quickly. (H) is correct because it rephrases the passage. The passage states that fictions *warp[s] our*

sense of reality (line 42), which is another way of saying that it *present[s] a distorted vision of the world.*

25. A

Start by looking for the key phrase "social skillfulness," which appears in line 64. The biggest mistake you could make here is to start there and keep reading. Instead, the fact that the sentence in which the phrase appears contains a dash indicates that you need to back up and read from the beginning of the sentence. If you do so, you'll find that the passage states *fiction-reading activates neuronal pathways in the brain that measurably help the reader better understand real human emotion.* In other words, its fiction builds social skills by changing the brain, making (A) the only possible answer.

26. J

If you have a good enough sense of the passage to know the author of Passage B only quotes writers to support her argument, you can eliminate (G). The author would not bother to mention those words if she believed that they were no longer relevant. (F) is unsupported by the passage: there is nothing to indicate that either James or Trollope changed public opinion. (H) is incorrect because while the author does mention Trollope to point out that he wrote about business in a way that remains relevant, there is nothing to indicate that either he or James "blurred" any lines between writing fiction and conducting business. (J) is correct because it is consistent with the author's overall point: fiction remains an accurate and relevant reflection of life.

27. A

The key to answering this question is to recognize that the question is asking about the second paragraph *in context*, and to consider that paragraph in context of the previous one. You can really think of this question as asking what changes between the first and second paragraphs. The fastest way to answer this question is to recognize that the author uses the word *I* (= personal experience) in the first paragraph but switches to the third-person in the second, making (A) correct. (B) is incorrect because the second paragraph does not even mention Keith Oatley's findings. This answer is completely off-topic. (C) is incorrect because both the second paragraph and the paragraph before it focus on the importance of literature. In fact, that is the focus of the entire passage. Science – the fact that reading activates pathways in the brain – is only mentioned because it supports the idea that reading literature is important. (D) is off-topic: there is no discussion of either contemporary or classic works in this paragraph. If you happen to know that Henry James is considered a classic author, don't get distracted: his actual works are not discussed.

28. G

What is the major similarity between the passages? Both authors make the point that fiction promotes empathy (Passage A: *Fiction enhances our ability to understand other people; it promotes a deep morality.* Passage B: fiction promotes theory of mind, *the ability to interpret and respond to those different from us*). Both of those statements directly correspond to the idea that fiction helps people see the world from "alternate perspectives." (F) is incorrect because only the author of Passage A would agree. (H) is incorrect because Passage A is clear that literature does not depict real life accurately. (J) is incorrect first because Passage A indicates that literature portrays the world as more fair than it actually is; and second because the author does not suggest that the "lie" is unreasonable (it *has important effects for society*).

29. D

If you think about the point of view from which each passage is written, this question can be quite straightforward. The key is to notice that the word *I* appears in Passage B but not in Passage A. By definition, then, the tone of Passage B is more personal and the tone of Passage A is less personal, i.e., more objective. (D) is therefore correct. All of the other answers indicate more emotion than is present in the passage.

30. G

What is the point of the quotation? That happy endings are not real, that they only exist in fairy tales. Which passage most directly conveys that idea? Passage A. Eliminate (F) and (G). Why? Because the author states that *fiction's happy endings seem to warp our sense of reality. They make us believe a lie: that the world is more just than it actually is* (lines 42-44). That is what (G) says, making it the answer.

Natural Science

31. C

If you feel like you've gotten bogged down in the details of the passage, look back at the beginning. Remember, the purpose of the introduction is to tell you what the passage is going to be about. In the second paragraph, Ralph Lorenz states *[The rocks] really are a curiosity…But I've always believed that this is something science could solve.* That line essentially tells you who the passage is about (Lorenz) and what he's trying to do (figure out how the rocks move). Note that the correct answer simply takes this idea and rephrases it in a more general way. A scientist = Lorenz, and a longstanding puzzle = how the rocks move. (A) is incorrect because although the passage does mention a couple of other theories about the rocks' movement, it does so in passing and never explicitly mentions any other scientists by name. (B) is flat-out untrue: the passage makes it clear that winds most likely do play a role in moving the rocks, even if there are other factors involved. And (D) is incorrect because again, the passage does not actually mention other scientists. Remember: whenever you see an answer choice stating a passage compares or contrasts multiple people, check to see how many people are actually mentioned by name. If there's only one, that answer cannot be true.

32. J

Start by reading the full sentence in which the word *hubcap* appears: *Watching the rocks travel is a bit like witnessing the rusting of a hubcap.* So the author is making a comparison between watching rocks and watching hubcaps rust. The question is why. To find the answer, you need to look before and after – unless you understand the allusion (rust forms very, very slowly), the sentence itself will not give you enough information. The sentence before indicates that observing the rocks was not easy (= difficult), and that the rocks moved "very rarely" (= slow). (F) and (G) are simply off-topic, and (H) extrapolates too far: the passage states that the researchers *weathered extreme temperatures*, but there is nothing to directly suggest that they were in danger.

142

33. B

If you're not sure where to start, do not try to reread the entire passage – when in doubt, look at the beginning and the end. Lorenz is introduced with the quote he believes *this is something science could solve*, and at the end of the passage, he states that *One day we'll figure all this out*. Both of these statements reveal his confident and optimistic attitude. Playing process of elimination, both (A) and (C) don't fit, and there is nothing to suggest Lorenz is amused, eliminating (D) as well.

34. G

Careful not to read too far into this question – the correct answer essentially rephrases the passage. Think about what the paragraph is saying: Lorenz believes that studying Racetrack Playa on Earth will help him better understand Titan. Why? Logically, because he can look at the effects of temperature changes on Earth's geology and use that information to make predictions about the effects of temperature changes on geology elsewhere in the universe. That would only be possible if temperature changes created the same geological effects on moons/planets other than Earth, which is what (G) says. (F) and (H) are both unsupported by the passage, but careful with (J): the phrase *that moon* refers to Titan, which the passage states is a moon of Saturn, not the Earth's moon. The passage says nothing about Earth's moon.

35. A

Start by considering the context. The passage is talking about a theory proposed by scientists, so the correct meaning must be consistent with that idea. What is a theory? Essentially, it's an argument in favor of a particular explanation, so (A) is correct. Otherwise, you know that *hold* will not be used in its literal meaning, so (B) can be eliminated. *Limits* and *grasps* simply do not make sense in context, again leaving (A).

36. H

Think about how the passage is arranged: the focus is on Lorenz and his theory about the rocks' movement, so you want to start by focusing on the place where his ideas are introduced. Although Lorenz is mentioned in the second paragraph, it isn't until the fourth paragraph that his ideas are presented – the third paragraph focuses on theories that are probably false. If you read the fourth paragraph carefully, you'll find the answer. Lines 37-43 indicate that the rocks are picked up by "ice collars," allowing the wind to carry them – which is what (H) says. Ideally, you should have circled the words *explained* (line 37) and *key* (line 41) as you skimmed through the passage – both of those are big tip-offs for important information. (F) is incorrect because rocks carried along by ice wouldn't leave trails (lines 28-29). Don't just pick this answer because you see the words *wind-driven sheets of ice* in lines 38-39 – the author is actually saying that this theory is incorrect (note the word *instead*). (G) is incorrect because the rocks move when friction is *reduced*, not because of the friction. And the information in (J) is never even mentioned in the passage.

37. B

The easiest way to answer this question is to recognize the play on words – the phrase *rock solid* is an idiom meaning "indisputable," but because the passage is literally about rocks, the author is punning on the word *rock* while pointing out that scientists don't yet have a reliable explanation for why the rocks move (= a shortcoming). If you don't get the humor, try process of elimination. (A) is incorrect because the statement does not *explain* anything – it's located next to the statement about a lack of strong winds at Racetrack Playa, but there's no relationship between the two ideas. (C) is incorrect because the scientific community *has* investigated the rocks – it just hasn't come up with a satisfying explanation for why they move. (D) is far too broad and extreme. The passage is about Lorenz and the Racetrack Playa rocks; there is nothing to support a statement about science as whole.

38. J

The primary challenge of this question lies in locating the answer; wind is mentioned multiple places in the passage. If you don't panic and start scanning the passage wildly, however, the question isn't that bad. Whenever a question asks about something that's discussed multiple places in the passage, you want to work through the references in order, from the beginning. The word *wind* first appears in the third paragraph, and if you read that paragraph carefully, you'll find the answer. Lines 25-28 state that in order to move the rocks, the Playa winds would have to be *100 miles per hour or more*, and since the winds can't move the rocks, they must blow at a speed lower than 100 miles per hour. (F) is incorrect because the passage does not state that winds *create* sailing ice – the two things are simply mentioned in the same paragraph, with no causal link between them. (G) is incorrect because winds do play a role in moving the rocks – they're just not the only factor. And (H) is incorrect because the moving rocks form trails, not the winds.

39. A

The key word is *experiment*, so start by looking for it. If you know that the passage is structured so that Lorenz's experiment is discussed last, you can start reading in the right-hand column. The key word appears in line 67. At this point, you have two options: you can either slog through the entire paragraph, or you can think about the big picture. Most of the paragraph is devoted to describing the specifics of the experiment, but the answer choices really just ask about its results – that means you want to focus on the end. (A) essentially rephrases the last sentence: even though the experiment was done in a very simple way, Lorenz got some very important results out of it. In (B), Titan has nothing to do with that experiment. (C) is incorrect because Lorenz didn't *conclusively* demonstrate anything – the experiment simply supported his theory. And (D) is incorrect because the experiment revealed nothing about basalt itself, only about how rocks could be made to move under a particular set of conditions.

40. G

The question asks for the "most convincing explanation," so you're going to look for a phrase that either contains those words or says something very similar. Consider also that the beginning of the passage focuses on describing the general mystery of the moving rocks and explaining why the existing explanations are lacking. It therefore makes sense to begin reading when the focus turns to Lorenz, in line 31. If you start there and skim for the key phrase, you'll find it in lines 60-61, which states that *ice rafting may be the best explanation for the trails we've been seeing*. The trails are left by the moving rocks, so (G) is correct. Ideally, you should have circled the words "best explanation" as you skimmed through the passage, regardless of whether you stopped to think about their importance – the word "explanation" will virtually always be significant, as will strong language such as "best." The two words paired together are something you should always mark.

Score Chart	
Raw Score	Scaled Score*
40	36
39	35
38	34
37	33
35	32
34	31
33	30
32	29
31	28
30	27
29	26
28	25
27	24
26	23
25	22
24	21
23	20
21-22	19
20	18
19	17
17-18	16
15-16	15
14	14
13	13
12	12
11	11
10	10
9	9
8	8
7	7
6	6
5	5
4	4
3	3
2	2
1	1
0	0

*Scaled scores are approximate and based on conversion charts from multiple administered exams.

Reprints and Permissions

Anaya, Rudolfo. *Bless Me Ultima*. New York: Hachette Book Group, 1994. p. 10.

Anft, Michael. "Solving the Mystery of Death Valley's Walking Rocks," *Johns Hopkins Magazine*, 6/1/11 (http://archive.magazine.jhu.edu/2011/06/solving-the-mystery-of-death-valley's-walking-rocks/). Reprinted by permission of *Johns Hopkins Magazine*.

de la Baume, Maïa. "That Instrument Known as the Eiffel Tower," *The New York Times*. 6/4/13. (http://www.nytimes.com/2013/06/05/arts/music/tower-music-from-eiffel-tower-by-joseph-bertolozzi.html)

Divakaruni, Chitra. "Writers on Writing: New Insights into the Novel? Try 300," *The New York Times*. 2/12/2001 (http://www.nytimes.com/2001/02/12/arts/12DIVA.html)

Excerpt from pp. 66-8 [780 words] from THE PAINTED DRUM by LOUISE ERDRICH. Copyright © 2005 by Louise Erdrich. Reprinted by permission of HarperCollins publishers.

Ferdinand, Marilyn. "Saving Grace," *Humanities*, March/April 2013, vol. 4, no. 32 (http://www.neh.gov/humanities/2013/marchapril/feature/saving-grace)

Excerpt from THINKING IN PICTURES by Temple Grandin, copyright © 1995, 2006 by Temple Grandin. Used by permission of Doubleday, an imprint of the Knopf Doubleday Publishing Group, a division of Random House, LLC. All rights reserved.

Gottschall, Jonathan. Excerpted from "Why Fiction is Good for You," *The Boston Globe*, 29 April 2012. (https://www.bostonglobe.com/ideas/2012/04/28/why-fiction-good-for-you-how-fiction-changes-your-world/nubDy1P3viDj2PuwGwb3KO/story.html). Reprinted by permission of the author.

Gray, Charlotte. "We Had No Idea What Alexander Graham Bell Sounded Like. Until Now." www.smithsonian.com, May 2013. (http://www.smithsonianmag.com/ist/?next=/history/we-had-no-idea-what-alexander-graham-bell-sounded-like-until-now-37585123/). Reprinted by permission of the author.

Heitman, Danny. "Ralph Waldo Emerson: Beyond the Greeting Cards," *Humanities*, May/June 2013, vol. 34, no. 3 (http://www.neh.gov/humanities/2013/mayjune/feature/ralph-waldo-emerson). Reprinted by permission of the author.

Koerth-Baker, Maggie. From "The Power of Positive Thinking, Truth or Myth?" *Live Science*, 29 August 2008, 5:20 AM, (http://www.livescience.com/2814-power-positive-thinking-truth-myth.html).

Kreamer, Anne. Adapted and condensed from "The Business Case for Reading Novels," Harvard Business Review Blog, 1/11/12. Original version available at http://blogs.hbr.org/2012/01/the-business-case-for-reading/). Reprinted by permission of the author.

Landau, Elizabeth. Adapted from "Why Happiness is Healthy," cnn.com, 3/20/14. http://www.cnn.com/2014/03/20/health/happiness-wellbeing-health/

Lehrer, Jonah. Adapted from "Under Pressure: The Search for Stress Vaccine," *Wired*, 7/28/10, 2:00p.m. http://www.wired.com/2010/07/ff_stress_cure/

Perrotet, Tony. "Where was the Birthplace of the American Vacation?" smithsonianmag.com, April 2013 (http://www.smithsonianmag.com/travel/where-was-the-birthplace-of-the-american-vacation-5520155/#ixzz2cQ5sp6ft). Reprinted by permission of the author.

Sainani, Kristin. Adapted from "What, Me Worry?" *Stanford Magazine*, May/June 2014. https://alumni.stanford.edu/get/page/magazine/article/?article_id=70134

Stromberg, Joseph. "For the First Time in 35 Years, a New Carnivorous Mammal Species is Discovered in the Americas," smithsonian.com, 8/15/13. (http://www.smithsonianmag.com/ist/?next=/science-nature/for-the-first-time-in-35-years-a-new-carnivorous-mammal-species-is-discovered-in-the-americas-48047/)

Styron, William. *Sophie's Choice*. New York: Random House, 1980. p. 3.

"Rules of the Game," from THE JOY LUCK CLUB by Amy Tan, copyright © 1989 by Amy Tan. Used by permission of G.P. Putnam's Sons, a division of Penguin Group (USA), LLC.

Tregaskis, Sharon. "The Buzz: What Bees Tell Us About Global Climate Change, *Johns Hopkins Magazine*, 6/2/2010. (http://archive.magazine.jhu.edu/2010/06/the-buzz-what-bees-tell-us-about-global-climate-change/) Reprinted with permission by *Johns Hopkins Magazine*.

Williford, James. "To Be or Not to Be," *Humanities*. January/February 2014, vol. 35, no. 1 (http://www.neh.gov/humanities/2014/januaryfebruary/feature/be-or-not-be)

ABOUT THE AUTHOR

Erica Meltzer earned her B.A. from Wellesley College and spent more than a decade tutoring privately in Boston and New York City, as well as nationally and internationally via Skype. Her experience working with students from a wide range of educational backgrounds and virtually every score level, from the third percentile to the 99th, gave her unique insight into the types of stumbling blocks students often encounter when preparing for standardized reading and writing tests.

She was inspired to begin writing her own test-prep materials in 2007, after visiting a local bookstore in search of additional practice questions for an SAT Writing student. Unable to find material that replicated the contents of the exam with sufficient accuracy, she decided to write her own. What started as a handful of exercises jotted down on a piece of paper became the basis for her first book, the original *Ultimate Guide to SAT Grammar*, published in 2011. Since that time, she has authored guides for SAT reading and vocabulary, as well as verbal guides for the ACT®, GRE®, and GMAT®. Her books have sold more than 100,000 copies and are used around the world. She lives in New York City, and you can visit her online at www.thecriticalreader.com.

Made in the USA
Lexington, KY
06 June 2019